Caught in the Net

The sequel to *Run For Your Wife*

A Comedy

Ray Cooney

Samuel French — London
New York - Toronto - Hollywood

CAUGHT IN THE NET

First produced at the Theatre Royal, Windsor, on 24th October, 2000, with the following cast:

Gavin Smith	William Harry
Vicki Smith	Katia Linden
Barbara Smith	Helen Gill
Mary Smith	Carol Hawkins
John Smith	Paul Nicholas
Stanley Gardner	Trevor Bannister
Dad	Ray Cooney

Directed by Ray Cooney
Designed by Douglas Heap

Subsequently produced by Bill Kenwright Ltd, at the Vaudeville Theatre, London, on 29th August, 2001, with the following cast:

Gavin Smith	William Harry
Vicki Smith	Beccy Armstrong
Barbara Smith	Helen Gill
Mary Smith	Carol Hawkins
John Smith	Robert Daws
Stanley Gardner	Russ Abbot
Dad	Eric Sykes

Directed by Ray Cooney
Designed by Douglas Heap

The action of the play takes place in the Wimbledon home of John and Mary Smith and, simultaneously, in the Streatham home of John and Barbara Smith

ACT I   Mid-afternoon on a warm summer's day
ACT II   Immediately following

Time — the present

AUTHOR'S NOTE

In the London production Mary's area UL, including the carpet, was blue. Barbara's area was yellow and the communal area was green (with the exception of Mary's phone which was blue and Barbara's phone which was yellow). The settee, armchairs and cushions in the communal area were of ranging shades of green. Again, in the London production, Mary's and Barbara's upstage areas were on a slightly raised level (approximately a nine inch rostrum) and there was a step down into the communal area.

Set design by Douglas Heap

Barbara (*to Gavin*) Gavin. I'm trying to take a shower.
Vicki (*calling towards the main bedroom*) Mum!
Barbara Your dad and I are going out tonight.
Gavin No, this is amazing.
Barbara Gavin!

Vicki moves to the kitchen door and opens it

Vicki (*calling into the kitchen*) Mum!
Gavin Won't take a second.

Gavin pulls Barbara to the settee

 Mary appears in the kitchen doorway. She is in her forties

Mary (*to Vicki*) I'm doing your dad's sandwiches.

Vicki pulls Mary to the settee

Vicki No, this is brilliant.
Mary He's got to be off in five minutes.
Barbara Dad'll be home in ten minutes.
Vicki Won't take a second.
Mary Honestly, Vicki!
Barbara Honestly, Gavin!

Gavin sits Barbara R of settee and Gavin sits on the R arm. At the same time Vicki sits Mary L of settee and Vicki sits on the L arm

Gavin (*to Barbara*) It's really unbelievable.
Vicki (*to Mary*) You're not going to believe this.
Gavin I've just signed off from Vicki.
Vicki I've just signed off from Gavin.
Barbara (*to Gavin*) Who's Vicki?
Mary (*to Vicki*) Who's Gavin?
Gavin ⎫
Vicki ⎭ (*together*) Mum!
Vicki I told you about Gavin.
Gavin You know Vicki Smith.
Vicki Gavin Smith.
Gavin ⎫
Vicki ⎭ (*together*) Oh, yes ——
Barbara You had an email from her.

Mary He sent you an email.

Gavin
Vicki } (*together*) Right!

Gavin Well, you know I said it was a bit of a coincidence ——

Vicki And I told you it was really funny, yeah ——

Gavin
Vicki } (*together*) That we were both called Smith.

Barbara Smith's a common name, Gavin.

Mary There's a lot of Smiths, Vicki.

Gavin Well —— !

Vicki Well —— !

Gavin
Vicki } (*together*) — today.

Gavin I started telling her about dad.

Vicki I got talking about dad.

Gavin It's just amazing.

Vicki It's really astonishing.

Mary
Barbara } (*together*) What is?

Gavin
Vicki } (*together*) What our dads have in common.

Gavin Look at this print-out!

Vicki Get a load of this, Mum!

Each hand their print-out to their mother

Gavin
Vicki } (*together*) Both called John!

Barbara Probably a million John Smiths in London.

Mary Thousands of John Smiths around.

Gavin
Vicki } (*together*) Middle name "Leonard"!

Barbara (*laughing*) Really?

Mary (*laughing*) That's good!

Gavin Hang on, it gets better ——

Vicki No, it's fantastic ——

Gavin Do you know how old Vicki's dad is?

Vicki How old do you reckon Gavin's dad is?

Mary and Barbara both shrug their shoulders

Gavin
Vicki } (*together*) Forty-three!

Barbara ⎱ (*together, laughing*) No!
Mary ⎰

Gavin ⎱ (*together*) Yeah!
Vicki ⎰

Gavin But the best bit is ——
Vicki But the greatest thing is
Barbara ⎱ (*together*) What?
Mary ⎰
Gavin Guess what Vicki's dad's job is?
Vicki Do you know what Gavin's dad does?

Gavin ⎱ (*together*) He's a taxi driver!
Vicki ⎰

Mary ⎱ (*together*) He's not!
Barbara ⎰

Gavin ⎱ (*together*) Yes, he is!
Vicki ⎰

Gavin We couldn't believe it!
Vicki I mean, what a coincidence.
Gavin There's Vicki's dad in Wimbledon.
Vicki Gavin's dad in Streatham ...

Gavin ⎱ (*together*) Same name.
Vicki ⎰

Gavin Drives a taxi ——
Vicki Taxi driver ——
Gavin Married with a kid ——
Vicki Married with a kid ——

Gavin ⎱ (*together*) — and both aged forty-three!
Vicki ⎰

Mary (*looking at her watch*) Yes, well, I've got to see your dad off.
Barbara (*looks at her watch*) Yes, well, I must get ready for your father
coming home.

Mary and Barbara rise simultaneously

Vicki Hold it a second, Mum ——
Gavin No, hang on, Mum. She's invited me round for tea.
Barbara (*scolding*) Gavin!
Vicki I've asked Gavin to come over.
Mary (*scolding*) Vicki!
Gavin OK, isn't it?
Vicki He sounds really nice.
Barbara You don't know anything about her, Gavin.
Gavin She sounds great.

Barbara
Mary } (*together*) You should have asked your father.
Gavin Come off it!
Vicki I'm fifteen, you know.
Gavin I'm sixteen, for God's sake.
Mary Better just check with him that it's OK.
Vicki It's only a cup of tea!
Barbara I've left the shower running.
Mary
Barbara } (*together*) Speak to your dad.

Barbara moves forwards to the main bedroom as Mary moves towards the kitchen

Gavin } (*together*) { Give over!
Vicki   { Honestly!

Vicki angrily throws herself into the armchair DL

Gavin puts his print-out on the table behind the settee, and moves towards his bedroom

Mary stops and turns

Mary He'll be leaving for his night shift in a minute.

Barbara opens the main bedroom door. She stops and turns to call after Gavin

Barbara He'll be home from his day shift in a minute!

Gavin exits into his bedroom

John Smith, a very ordinary but cheery man in his forties, comes in from the main bedroom as Barbara exits into the main bedroom — as John is in Wimbledon and Barbara is in Streatham they don't react to one another

John (*as he enters; to Mary, brightly*) Right, I'm off, sweetheart.
Mary I'll get your sandwiches. Cheese and pickle and ham. Oo ... a packet of crisps. And a slice of that cream cake.
John Yummy, yummy!
Mary (*to Vicki*) Go on, ask Dad.
Vicki Honestly, Mum, you'd think it was a drugs and sex orgy.
John What's that, the latest TV sitcom?
Mary (*to Vicki*) Ask him!

Mary exits into kitchen

John (*to Vicki*) Ask me what?
Vicki It's a boy I met on the Internet.
John It's not good for your eyesight all that computer stuff.
Vicki I told you about him, remember?
John Did you?
Vicki You know I did! Pretty amazing. We're both called "Smith".
John Oh, yes. (*Sarcastically*) Astonishing. Two Smiths!

During the ensuing dialogue John gets his jacket from the cupboard, UL and puts it on

Vicki Well, it got even better.
John Got better, did it? Good. What did?
Vicki The coincidence. Now, there must be — what — at least one hundred and twenty-five thousand "Smiths" in the London area, yeah?
John At least. If I'm not awake when you leave for school in the morning, come in and give me a great big hug.

John kisses Vicki and moves to the kitchen

Vicki Well, this is the brilliant bit, Dad. Of the one hundred and twenty-five thousand "Smiths" in the London area ——
John London area, yeah.

John opens the kitchen door

(*Calling through*) Mary, don't forget the KitKat and the Mars Bar.
Vicki — the boy I logged on to has a father who's called John Leonard Smith and drives a taxi.

John turns from Vicki to close the door then realizes what she's said. There is a pause then John, still with his back to Vicki, closes the kitchen door

He only lives in Streatham.

John turns: his face blank. He then emits a foolish laugh

And you're both aged forty-three!

There is a pause as John's mind whirls — then he emits another foolish laugh

And we met surfing the Internet.

She holds out the print-out. John hesitates then, dumbly, takes it

Isn't that the most amazing coincidence?
John (*laughing*) Amazing! (*He walks past her scrutinizing the print-out*)
Vicki And Streatham's just round the corner!
John Yes!
Vicki Wicked, isn't it? Me in Wimbledon. Gavin in Streatham.
John You in — er — and — er — Gavin in — er ——
Vicki Streatham, yeah!
John And — er — you and — er — Gavin have been — er — on the — er
—— (*He indicates the print-out*)
Vicki On the Internet. He's sixteen and he sounds pretty sexy.
John No, he's not! I mean — er — he's probably not.
Vicki He sounds it. Really cool.
John No, he isn't! I forbid it!
Vicki Forbid what?
John Everything. What you've been doing.
Vicki We haven't been doing anything.
John Yes, and it's got to stop.
Vicki (*perplexed*) What has?
John What you're doing. On the Internet. All this swimming — surfing!
Vicki Don't be daft! (*She takes back the print-out and sits in armchair* DRC)
John I won't have it! Logging on to strangers!
Vicki Have you flipped?
John No, I have not flipped! I knew those machines were dangerous. Full
of weirdos and cranks.
Vicki Gavin's not a weirdo!
John Yes, he is! I'm not having my daughter getting involved with weirds
and crankos!

Mary enters with a lunch-box

Mary Sandwiches!
John (*jumping*) Ahh!
Mary You all right, precious?

John adopts a light-hearted attitude

John Fine. You can leave this to me. I'll sort it out.
Mary Sort what out?

John pushes Mary towards the kitchen

John Nothing. There's nothing to sort out. Just go back into the kitchen, please.

Vicki Dad's totally lost it.

John I have not lost it.

Mary Lost what?

Mary crosses in front of John, searching. John pulls her back across him

John Will you please go into the kitchen!

Mary I've finished in the kitchen. (*She hands John the lunch-box*)

John I want more than this. We've got some of that Indian left over left over, haven't we? (*He thrusts the box back at Mary*)

Vicki rises

Vicki (*to Mary*) Mum, tell him I can see Gavin!

John (*to Vicki*) This is nothing to do with your mother.

Mary I said it was best to ask if he could come round.

John Mary, will you please — (*realizing*) come round? Who's coming round?

Vicki I don't know what you're getting so excited about.

Mary (*to John*) The young Smith boy's coming over for tea that's all.

John (*to Mary; mortified*) From Streatham?

Vicki Yes.

John (*to Vicki; mortified*) To Wimbledon?

Vicki Yes.

John How did he get our address?

Vicki How do you think? I emailed it to him.

John (*ashen*) You gave him our address?

Vicki Yes.

John (*hoarsely*) In Wimbledon.

Mary That's where we live, John.

Vicki He's coming between four and five.

John (*to Vicki*) Ring him up.

Vicki What?

John Tell him not to come.

Vicki Why?

John Because I say so.

Mary It's not all that serious is it, Johnny?

John It's bloody serious! (*He pushes Mary towards the kitchen*)

Mary I thought it was pretty interesting really. Another taxi driver called John Leonard Smith.

John I don't find that interesting. I find that totally boring.

Mary Both aged forty-three!
John Totally bloody boring! (*To Vicki*) You're not getting involved with him and that's that.
Vicki All I'm doing is giving the bloke a cup of tea.
John Yes, that's how it starts. (*He moves to the telephone L of the settee*) Ring him up now and tell him not to come.
Vicki I won't!
John All right. I'll ring him up. (*He lifts the receiver*)
Vicki You don't know his number.

There is a very brief pause

John You're right, I don't. (*He replaces the receiver and carries the phone to Vicki*) You ring him up.
Mary I think you're being a bit unreasonable, John.
Vicki (*sitting in armchair* DRC) Bloody unreasonable!
John (*to Vicki*) You mind your bloody language, young lady. (*To Mary*) I'm not having *that* boy in *this* house.
Mary For heaven's sake!
John I'm not having our daughter subjected to the whims of an on-line sexual deviant!
Vicki What?!
John Now you call him immediately and say if he pesters you any more your father will put the police on to him.
Mary You go and do your night shift ——
John I'm not going anywhere until this is sorted out.
Vicki (*angry but tearful*) It's sorted! He's coming over!
John Vicki, go to your room.
Vicki Come off it!
John Go to your room this instant!
Vicki (*rising; crying*) You're a great big bully!

Mary runs past John to Vicki

Mary It's all right, sweetheart. (*To John*) I'm sure you're wrong about the boy. (*To Vicki*) What's his name again?
Vicki (*still crying; confused*) What? I don't know. *Gary.*
John It's *Gavin!* (*Realizing*) It doesn't matter what his name is! (*To Mary*) And I'm not wrong about him! He should be doing his homework instead of pestering the one hundred and twenty-five thousand Smiths who live in the London area.
Mary Really, John ——

Gavin enters from the second bedroom

Gavin (*calling*) Mum!
John I'm the man of the house here and I say who's welcome and who isn't.
And that sexual pervert is not welcome!

Gavin closes his door and opens the second bedroom door

Gavin Mum!

Vicki bursts into tears and runs towards the second bedroom

Barbara, in dressing-gown and slippers enters from the main bedroom

During the following, John replaces the phone on the table L of the settee

Vicki Oh, Dad.
Mary (*running towards the departing Vicki*) Vicki!
Barbara What now?
Gavin Is Dad back?
Barbara No, he's not. He's late, too.

Vicki goes into the bedroom and slams the door

Mary (*to John, testily*) Do you really want to take the Indian left over?
John (*moving towards Mary*) Yes, I do!

John propels Mary towards the kitchen

Gavin Well, I'm going round to Vicki's place, you tell Dad.
Barbara No. Wait and ask your father. He'll be home any minute now. And
Gavin, I'm trying to get ready.
Mary You're being a real pain today, John.
Gavin You're being a real pain today, Mum.

*Gavin slumps off into the second bedroom as Barbara exits into the main
bedroom and Mary exits into the kitchen*

John slams the kitchen door and leans his back on it

John Oh, my God! (*He quickly takes out his mobile phone and dials*) You
wretched boy, Gavin!

The phone in Streatham rings

Come on, Barbara, come on!

*The Wimbledon front doorbell rings. John looks towards the front door in
horror*

Oh—my — God!!! It's Gavin!

*Barbara, now dressed in a towel, runs in from the bedroom and moves to
phone*

*John shuts the mobile and puts it in his trousers pocket as Barbara reaches
the phone. The Wimbledon doorbell rings again. John dithers not knowing
what to do*

Barbara (*into the phone*) Hallo?!

John hurries to open the kitchen door

(*Into the phone*) Hallo?!
John (*calling through the door*) I'll get it!
Barbara (*into the phone*) Hallo?!!

*John slams the kitchen door closed and hurriedly tiptoes towards the front
door to listen*

*Vicki enters from the second bedroom. She watches John for a brief
moment*

Vicki Dad ——!
John (*yelling*) Ahh! Vicki! Go to your room.
Vicki If that's Gavin for me ——
Barbara (*into the phone*) Hallo!
John I'll deal with Gavin! Go to your room, this instant!
Barbara OO!
Vicki OO!

*Barbara slams the phone down and exits into main bedroom as Vicki exits
into the second bedroom, both slamming the doors*

The Wimbledon doorbell rings

John Wretched boy!

*John quickly turns the key in Vicki's bedroom lock. He grabs an anorak from
the cupboard UL and puts it on. He pulls the hood completely over his head
to hide his face. The Wimbledon doorbell rings again. John edges towards
the front door*

Mary enters from kitchen with the lunch-box

Mary (*as she enters*) John!

John freezes with his back to Mary

John (*turning*) Yep!

Mary is surprised to be confronted by John totally enveloped in the anorak

Mary What on earth are you doing?
John I felt chilly. (*He moves down a pace away from the front door*)
Mary It's about seventy degrees out there.
John I think I've got a cold coming on. (*He moves down another pace*)

Mary steps towards John

Mary Well, there's your supper. That'll do you good. (*She hands him the lunch-box*)
John Where's my Indian left over?!
Mary (*indicating the box*) I've given it to you!
John Well, where's my drink?
Mary Can of Coke in your box.
John Coke?! I want tea.
Mary Tea? You never take tea.
John I want tea today. And some of your soup. (*He starts to push Mary towards the kitchen*)

Mary stops

Mary Soup?
John Yes, some of your super soup. Super soup.

John pushes Mary but she stops again

Mary Hang on a second. Didn't I hear the doorbell go just now?
John No. (*He turns to Mary*)

The front doorbell rings again. Mary turns back

  Maybe you did.
Mary It might be that Gavin.
John If it is I'll get rid of him.

Mary Don't do anything stupid!
John You leave that nasty little pervert to me! (*He pushes Mary towards the kitchen*)

Mary is pushed into the kitchen

John slams the kitchen door closed

John puts the lunch-box on the table, UL. *The doorbell rings again. He makes sure that the anorak hood is completely masking his face. He then opens the door about a foot and turns his back to the door*

(*Disguising his voice with a thick German accent*) Go away young man. Zis is Herr Schmidt! You are not velcome here! My family vish to have nuzzing to do viz you!

Stanley Gardner, aged in his forties, slowly edges through the door clutching two large shopping bags. He looks bewildered. Stanley is a "good soul" but not overly bright

John, averting his face, continues the Germanic diatribe which gets increasingly manic

Zis is private property and I demand zat you leave ze premises immediately. Failure to remove yourself vill result in unpleasant force being perpetrated upon your person. Go — now! Und never darken our doorsteps again!
Stanley (*firmly*) Is that from *Saving Private Ryan*?

John slowly turns to Stanley, then throws off his hood

John Stanley, it's you!
Stanley Couldn't find my keys. (*Indicating the anorak*) You got a cold coming on?
John Yes! And it could develop into double pneumonia.

John pulls Stanley down a pace and slams the door

Stanley Why, what's up then?
John Disaster!
Stanley Oh, dear. I'll just nip up to the flat, dump this lot, then you can tell me about it.
John There's no time.

Stanley crosses John to go upstairs

Stanley Won't take a second. I'll unpack the ——

John pulls Stanley to DL *of the settee*

John Stanley! I'm going to need your help.
Stanley John, you know me. Always willing to lend a ——
John (*interrupting*) Yes, I know you are. (*He takes out his mobile while continuing to talk*) I've got to make a very important phone call.
Stanley Important phone call.
John (*pressing on*) But it's going to be safer to make it when I'm in my taxi ——
Stanley In your taxi.
John (*pressing on*) So I'm going to leave you holding the fort.
Stanley Holding the fort.
John Will you stop interrupting and *listen*.

Mary enters from the kitchen with a flask of tea and a flask of soup

John quickly puts the mobile into a pocket of the anorak

Mary (*as she enters*) Was that Vicki's young ——? (*She sees Stanley; tersely*) Oh, it's *you*, Stanley. (*She angrily bangs the kitchen door shut*)
Stanley Yes, your favourite lodger.
Mary I don't know what gives you that idea.
Stanley (*chuckling*) Mary!

John pulls Stanley across him and moves to Mary

John (*to Mary*) You're making me tea, Mary.
Mary I've *made* it. Soup. Tea. (*She thrusts the flasks at him*)
John No, I want a *cup. Now.*
Mary Well pour one from that! (*She points to flask*)
John No. That's for the road. I want a nice cup of your lovely special "Johnny-I-love-you" cups.
Mary Can't you make your own cup?
John No, Stanley wants to talk to me, don't you?

Before the bemused Stanley can reply John presses on

And it's private, Mary. He's got this very personal emotional problem, haven't you?

Before the bemused Stanley can reply John presses on

(*To Mary*) And he needs my advice.

John tries to push Mary to the kitchen but she returns to Stanley

Mary Advice on how to get a job would be more useful.
Stanley Now, Mary, if you're worried that I haven't paid this month's rent
    yet ——
John She isn't!
Mary No, I'm not worried about this month's rent.
John I told you.
Stanley Oh, good.
Mary It's last month's and the month's before.
Stanley Now, Mary. We can discuss this ——
John Discuss it later. You make the tea while I sort out Stanley's personal
    emotional problem.

John opens the kitchen door for Mary

Stanley (*to John*) Considering I've been a lodger here for nearly eighteen
    years, I think Mary's being very unreasonable.
John It doesn't matter!
Mary You've been a lodger for eighteen years and paid the rent for about
    ten.
John Mary ——!
Stanley I might have missed the odd month.
John Stanley ——!
Mary You're dead right. You pay the rent on the even months and miss the
    odd ones.
John Will you make the tea please! (*He pushes Mary towards the kitchen*)

Mary is pushed into the kitchen

John slams the kitchen door

    (*To Stanley*) Now, listen ——

Mary returns

Mary And another thing —— (*She bangs the kitchen door shut*)
John God!

John breaks, puts the flasks down on the table behind the settee and continues
R, *removing his anorak*

Mary (*to Stanley*) I thought you were going on holiday today.

Stanley I am. I've just been shopping for the trip, organizing myself for the delights of Felixstowe. (*He puts the shopping bags on the settee and sits*)

John puts his anorak on chair DR *and moves* DRC

John (*interrupting*) Forget Felixstowe!

Stanley (*starting to remove some of the holiday items, pressing on*) Sun hat, sun cream, mosquito repellent, Imodium Plus ——

John We don't need an inventory, Stanley.

Stanley Snorkel, mask, water wings. It's never too late to learn, you know.

Mary I hope you've left your flat tidy.

Stanley (*proudly*) You know me, Mary.

Mary (*flatly*) Yes. I hope you've left your flat tidy.

John Please, Mary! Make the tea! This personal emotional problem of his is very pressing!

Mary If he got himself a wife and moved out of our house *all* his personal and emotional problems might be solved.

Stanley (*rising*) I don't have a personal emotional problem!

John (*to Mary*) It's more of an intimate sexual problem, actually.

Mary Oh. (*To Stanley*) I suppose you want a cup of tea as well, do you?

John No, he doesn't want a cup! (*To Stanley*) Do you?!

Stanley Better not. I'm leaving in about ten or fifteen minutes and I don't want to be caught short on the motorway. Although, I'm picking Dad up from Clapham first — he's coming with me to Felixstowe — he loves it there ... So, I could always spend a penny while I'm in Clapham — I must make sure Dad spends one, too, with his bladder and that journey, and he's getting very forgetful these days. Only last week in the High Street ——

John Shut up! (*To Mary*) Just make the tea! (*He pushes Mary off*)

Mary exits

Stanley, I've got to be brief and very fast!

Stanley Fine by me, John.

John Our Vicki's found out about me and Barbara.

Stanley Who's Barbara?

John Barbara, Streatham!

Stanley (*thinking*) Barbara Streatham. No. Name doesn't ring a bell.

John Barbara *Smith*!

Stanley No, I can't say I know a Barbara ... (*Realizing*) Smith?!

John Ssh!

Stanley, mortified, crosses John and points to kitchen

Stanley You mean your other ——? (*He indicates his wedding ring finger*)
John (*interrupting*) Yes! Vicki's found out about Gavin, too!
Stanley (*aghast*) When you say, "Gavin", you mean ——?! (*He indicates the height of a young boy*)
John Yes!
Stanley Ahhh!
John Well, she doesn't know she's found out but she has. She's invited him round for tea. (*He feels his pockets*) What did I do with my mobile?
Stanley (*aghast*) Your son's coming over to Wimbledon?
John She met him in that computer of hers.
Stanley (*confused*) Met him where?
John Through that Internet thing.
Stanley Bloody hell!
John Two million subscribers and my stupid daughter has to log on to my stupid son. Where the hell is my mobile? (*He starts to look around the room, moving* ULC)
Stanley I told you ages ago you couldn't get away with this double life forever.
John I've got away with it for eighteen years.

Stanley moves URC *to John*

Stanley Bigamy is still a criminal offence, you know.
John I don't want a sermon, Stanley!
Stanley "He who dares to tell a lie — 'Shall be smitten.'"
John Shut up! Where is it?
Stanley (*pointing to the Wimbledon phone*) Why don't you use *that* phone?
John Don't be daft. I never use the home phone here or in Streatham.
Stanley Why not?
John Too dangerous. I always use the mobile to call Mary or Barbara.
Stanley (*in awe*) Blimey!
John Where the hell is it? If it's not too late, I've got to stop Gavin leaving the house. (*Realizing*) Of course! I put it in my anorak.

John pushes past Stanley, grabs his mobile from his anorak and, during the ensuing dialogue, dials. He moves DR *of the armchair as Stanley moves* UL *of it*

Stanley, if those two kids meet the truth is bound to come out. Mary and Barbara will be mortified. Vicki and Gavin horrified. As for me ——
Stanley Petrified.

John Bloody crucified.

John thrusts the anorak on to Stanley who throws it on to the back of the settee

The Streatham phone rings

It's ringing. I've got to go. If I miss Gavin in Streatham and he turns up here, get rid of him. (*Into the mobile*) Come on, Barbara.

John moves DS *of the armchair to run out. Stanley hurries above the settee and they meet* ULC

Stanley What do you mean get rid of him?
John That's where *you* come in. (*To Stanley*) Don't let Gavin in the house!
Stanley I'm taking Dad to Felixstowe!

There is loud banging from the second bedroom door

Vicki (*off*) Hey!

Stanley looks to John

John Ignore it.

There are more bangs

Vicki Hey, Dad!
Stanley Is that your Vicki?
John I've locked her in.
Stanley Bloody hell!
Vicki (*off*) Let me out, you stupid, stupid man!
Stanley I think she's getting cross.

Gavin enters from the second bedroom, shutting the door. He gets a motorbike jacket from the hallstand

John (*calling to Vicki*) Won't be a moment, sweetheart. I'm looking for the key. Thanks, Stan, you're a real pal. (*With the mobile to his ear, he turns to go*)

Stanley grabs him

Stanley Hold it!

Gavin (*calling*) Mum! The phone's ringing.
John Why isn't Barbara answering?

Stanley marches John DLC

Stanley I need instructions!
Gavin (*opening the main bedroom door*) Mum, phone!
John I've given you instructions. Don't let Gavin in the house.

As John moves to go Stanley grabs him

> *Barbara enters from the main bedroom and heads for the phone. She is now*
> *dressed in a towelling dressing-gown*

Gavin moves to the mirror between the bedroom doors and checks his
appearance

Barbara (*as she enters*) Are you incapable of answering the phone, Gavin?
Stanley What if he won't take "no" for an answer?!
Barbara (*into the phone*) Hallo?!

John goes to speak

> *Mary enters from the kitchen carrying a mug of tea*

Mary One tea!

As Mary turns to close the door John neatly throws his mobile over his
shoulder to Stanley who, equally neatly, throws it over his shoulder. It lands
on the settee amongst Stanley's packages. John sits down on the arm of the
chair DL *and Stanley sits down on the* L *arm of the settee. Mary turns back to*
be confronted by John and Stanley looking relaxed and totally innocent.
Mary crosses to Stanley

   (*To Stanley*) You still here?
Stanley Er — yes.
John (*rising*) Yes. His sexual problem is bigger than I thought.
Barbara (*into the phone*) Hallo!

Mary hands John his tea

Mary There's your tea.
John Where's Stanley's tea?

Mary He said he didn't want one.

John pulls Mary across him

John He's changed his mind, he's desperate for one.

John pushes Mary off into the kitchen

   Mary exits

Barbara Hallo?
Gavin (*turning from the mirror*) Is it Dad?
Barbara Ssh! Hallo!!
John (*to Stanley*) Where's my mobile?
Stanley I threw it over my shoulder.
John Why the hell did you do that?
Stanley Because that's what *you* did!
John Twit! Quick!

John puts his mug of tea on the table behind the settee as they frantically start to search for the mobile behind the settee

Barbara (*into the phone*) OO! (*She angrily bangs the phone down and heads for the main bedroom*)
Gavin Who was it?
Barbara God knows!
Gavin I'm not waiting for Dad any longer. Tell him I've gone round to Vicki's place.
Barbara Hang on! I'd better ring her mother and say you're coming over.
Gavin Please yourself. Their phone number's on this print-out. (*He hands her the print-out and heads for the front door*)
Barbara You going on your motorbike?
Gavin (*in the doorway*) Yes, I know, drive carefully!

   Gavin exits through the front door

Barbara checks the print-out and Stanley finds John's mobile

Stanley One mobile!
John (*grabbing the mobile*) Numbskull! You're in charge, Stan.
Stanley I'm collecting Dad from Clapham.
John You're staying here in case Gavin arrives. "Re-dial"!

John hits the re-dial key as Barbara starts to dial

Vicki (*off*) Dad! Have you found that key?!
John (*calling*) Very nearly! (*He starts to move but stops*) Hell, it's engaged!
   I'd better get round there quick.
Stanley John!

*John hits the off key, puts the mobile in his pocket and starts to move as the
Wimbledon phone rings. John quickly picks up the phone*

John (*into the phone*) Yeah?
Barbara (*into the phone*) My name's Barbara Smith.
John (*with a strangled cry*) Ooo!! (*He removes the phone from his ear and
   looks at it, horrified*)
Barbara (*into the phone*) Hallo?
Stanley (*to John*) What's the matter?
Barbara (*into the phone*) Can I speak to Vicki's mother or father please?
John (*with a strangled cry*) Ooo!! (*In one movement he removes the phone
   from his ear, looks at it horrified, and returns it to his ear*)
Barbara (*into the phone*) Hallo!
John (*finally, into the phone; in a Chinese accent*) Hallo, this is Blue Dragon
   Chinese restaurant.

Barbara looks surprised. Stanley looks amazed

   (*In a Chinese accent*) Can I help you, please?
Barbara (*into the phone; confused*) Do Mr and Mrs Smith live there?
John (*into the phone, in a Chinese accent; with false anger*) No, this Blue
   Dragon! Mr and Mrs Hung Lo. (*To Stanley*) It's Barbara!
Stanley Barbara!

*Carrying both receiver and cradle, John moves to DC of the settee to get away
from the kitchen. Stanley moves down to John's left*

John (*into the phone, in a Chinese accent*) And you no ring this number
   again! We no do take-away.

Barbara sits in the chair L

Barbara (*into the phone*) I'm sorry!

*Mary comes in from the kitchen carrying a mug of tea. She stops on seeing
John on the phone talking in a Chinese accent*

John is oblivious to Mary. She walks slowly to Stanley's L

John (*into the phone; in a Chinese accent*) We no believe in take-away! This telephone number only for our personal customers. No riffraff. We do very special Chinese food here. Excellent Peking duck. Chop suey with soy sauce ——

Barbara (*into the phone*) Could you tell me what your telephone number is, please?

John No! We do sweet and sour fish. Sweet and sour pork. Sweet and sour duck. Crispy noodles. We have very extensive menu ... .

Stanley sees Mary, smiles and taps John on the shoulder. John shrugs him away and presses on

Barbara (*into the phone*) I'm sure I dialled the right number ——
John (*interrupting*) We also do fried rice, boiled rice, spicy rice.

Stanley tugs at John's sleeve. John pulls away and carries on. Mary crosses to John, intrigued

(*Into the phone; in a Chinese accent*) And also poppadoms, chapati and vindaloo —— (*He sees Mary*) OO! Ah, so! (*Into the phone; in a Chinese accent*) And he be round to collect it right way. (*He replaces the receiver; to Mary*) She only understands Chinese.

John hands Mary the telephone. Mary thrusts the telephone on to Stanley. A confused Barbara switches off her phone. Stanley moves ULC *and puts the phone on the table* L *of settee, as John pushes Mary towards the kitchen*

(*To Mary*) Stanley's taking a Chinese for him and his dad to eat on the way to Felixstowe. Love Chinese, don't you, Stan, and your dad?
Stanley (*flatly*) Love it.

During the following, Barbara rises, checks the telephone number on the print-out and dials again. Mary crosses John to Stanley

Mary (*to Stanley*) Here's your tea. (*Flatly*) It's India not China.
Stanley (*taking the mug*) Lovely.
John I've got to get going!

There is a banging from the second bedroom

Vicki (*off*) Hey! Have you found that key?!

John (*to Mary*) Don't let her out until she promises never to contact Gavin again.
Mary Really, John!
John You make her promise! And don't take her word. Get her to sign something. I've got to go! (*He pulls Mary across him and starts to go*)

Mary picks up John's lunch-box from the table ULC

Mary What about your supper?
John I won't have time ——! (*Quickly*) Of course, I will! (*He takes the lunch-box*)

The Wimbledon telephone rings. John and Stanley look at it, look at each other, look to Mary, look back to each other, then look back to Mary and laugh foolishly

Gavin hurries in from the Streatham front door

Gavin Mum, have you seen my crash helmet?
Barbara (*furiously waiting for the phone to be answered*) In the hallstand, I think.

Gavin goes up and looks in the hallstand chest UR

Mary (*to John*) Well, aren't you going to answer it?
John Yes. (*He lifts the receiver; into the phone*) Yep?
Barbara (*into the phone*) Is this the right number for Mr John Smith?

John thinks for a very brief second and replaces the receiver

(*Angrily*) OO!

During the following Barbara dials again

Mary (*to John*) Why did you do that?
John It was a heavy breather.
Mary Heavy breather?
John It's happened several times. Very upsetting. You've had it, haven't you, Stanley?
Stanley (*pointedly*) Yes, I've had it!

Gavin moves from the hallstand and towards the second bedroom

Gavin (*as he goes*) Must be in my bedroom.

Gavin exits into the second bedroom

John I've got to go!

The Wimbledon phone rings. John and Stanley look to each other. An angry Mary goes to answer it

Mary For heaven's sake!
Stanley ⎤ (*together*) No!!
John ⎦
Mary (*jumping*) Ah!
John (*to Mary*) It could be him again. You know —— (*He does quick heavy breathing then grabs the phone to his ear*)
Barbara (*into the phone*) Hallo!

John immediately bangs the phone down. During the following dialogue a furious Barbara checks the print-out and dials once more

John (*to Mary*) It was him again. Disgusting! Don't you find him disgusting, Stanley?
Stanley (*at a loss*) I think I feel sorry for him, actually.

John takes Mary to the second bedroom

John (*to Mary*) Look, it might be a good idea, darling, if you went and comforted Vicki. Let Stanley guard the telephone, eh? I really must get going. (*To Stanley*) If that heavy breather rings again just slam the phone down. And if that pervert Gavin turns up march him round to the nearest police station.

John opens the front door and picks up his two flasks from the table behind the settee

Stanley What about my poor old normal dad in Clapham?!
John He'll keep!

The Wimbledon phone rings. John hesitates then picks it up. He does some quick heavy breathing into the receiver and slams it down

(*To Mary*) See how they like it!

John rushes out through the front door

Stanley (*calling after him*) John! JOHN!

During the following dialogue, a fuming Barbara dials again. Vicki bangs on the door

Vicki (*off*) Have you found that bloody key?!

Mary moves to Vicki's bedroom

Mary (*calls*) It's all right, sweetie! (*To Stanley*) If you've finished your tea, you can pick up your father and push off to Felixstowe.
Stanley (*dithering*) I'm not quite sure ——
Mary Well, I am!

Mary unlocks Vicki's bedroom door

> *Vicki, angry and tearful, storms in*

Vicki Where's that stupid father of mine?!
Mary He's left for his night shift.

Vicki sees Stanley

Vicki Oh, hallo, Uncle Stan. I thought you were going on holiday to Felixstowe with your dad.
Stanley So did I!
Mary (*pointedly*) Stanley's just leaving.

Stanley gives Vicki a little wave. The Wimbledon telephone rings. Stanley looks at it, horrified. Mary moves towards the phone but Stanley rushes to it and picks it up. Mary looks surprised and Stanley stares at her. He then breathes heavily into the phone and slams it down. Stanley proudly looks at Mary

Stanley (*defiantly raising his fist*) Yes!
Barbara OO!

> *Barbara storms off into the main bedroom with the phone, leaving the print-out on the table*

During the following, Stanley looks out of the front door in case Gavin arrives

Vicki (*blankly*) Why did Uncle Stan do that, Mum?

Mary Why does Uncle Stanley do anything? You go and bathe your eyes. Mummy will get you an aspirin.

Vicki (*defiantly*) I'm seeing Gavin when he arrives!

Mary Of course you are.

Stanley closes the front door and looks through the letter-box of the closed front door

Vicki exits into the second bedroom

Mary heads towards the kitchen but stops to glare at Stanley

(*Pointedly to Stanley*) Goodbye, Stanley!

Stanley I've been thinking about Vicki and Gavin ——

Mary (*sternly*) Have a nice holiday, Stanley!

Stanley moves DLC

Stanley Er — Mary, if Gavin is a sexual pervert I really don't think ——

Mary (*interrupting*) Stanley! If I were you I'd forget other people's sexual problems and concentrate on your own!

Mary exits into kitchen

Stanley sits on the chair, DL

Stanley Well, nice way to start a holiday. (*He takes a swig of his tea*)

John rushes in from the front door

John Stanley!

Stanley (*spluttering tea*) Ahh! Please, don't do that.

John moves DLC

John Would you believe it!

Stanley (*rising*) What's happened?!

John Half a minute down the road and the bloody taxi gets a puncture! Give me the keys to your car.

Stanley Eh?

John I've got to get over to Streatham. Now!

Stanley I need my car. I'm taking Dad to Felixstowe!

Barbara enters dialling on her phone, closing her door. She moves to R *of the settee and sits on the arm*

John I'll be back in twenty minutes. Give me the keys!
Stanley Bloody hell.

Stanley gives John his mug and starts to feel for his car keys

Gavin enters from the second bedroom carrying his crash helmet

Gavin Found it! Who are you calling? (*He looks in the mirror* URC *and during the following secures his helmet*)
Barbara Your father on his mobile. It's so unlike him to be late.
John (*to Stanley*) Come on! Come on!
Stanley All right, all right!

Before Stanley finds his car keys, John's mobile rings a merry march tune

What the hell's that?
John My mobile.

John hands Stanley the mug and grabs the mobile out of his pocket. Stanley puts the mug on the table ULC

(*Into the mobile*) Yeah?
Barbara (*into the phone*) Johnny! Where are you, pumpkin?
John (*relieved, into the phone*) Thank heavens! My little boobie boo-boos!

Stanley turns

Stanley Boobie boo-boos??
John It's Barbara.
Stanley Barbara?!
John (*to Stanley*) Where the hell are your car keys?
Stanley I can't find them!
John God!
Gavin (*turning from the mirror*) Dad OK?
Barbara I think so, yes.
John Where's Mary?
Stanley In the kitchen.

Barbara rises and, during the following, moves above the settee and sits on the L *arm of the settee*

Barbara (*into the phone*) You there, Johnny?
John (*into the mobile*) Yes, pumpkin. I'm in the taxi on the way home.

Stanley Bloody hell!
John (*to Stanley*) Keep Mary out of here for a minute!

John starts to push a resisting Stanley towards the kitchen

Stanley What? How?
Barbara (*into the phone*) Johnny!
John (*into the mobile*) Sorry, darling. I keep losing you. (*To Stanley*) Tell her a funny story!
Stanley I don't think I know any ——
John (*interrupting*) Make one up!
Barbara (*into the phone*) You there, Johnny?
John (*into the mobile*) I lost you again. I'm in the Blackwall Tunnel.

John opens the kitchen door

Stanley Blimey, it's like a James Bond movie.

John pushes Stanley into the kitchen and slams the door

Eyeing the kitchen, John moves to DC of the settee

John (*into the mobile*) I'm out now! I've been trying to phone you for ages. Where's Gavin?!
Barbara (*into the phone*) I'm not surprised you couldn't get through. I've had the most crazy telephone calls.
John (*into the mobile*) Yes, where's Gavin?! Is he there?
Barbara (*into the phone*) I've had three wrong numbers, two heavy breathers and a Chinese restaurant.
Gavin (*to Barbara*) Bye, Mum.

Barbara rises

Barbara Bye.
John (*into the mobile*) Barbara!
Gavin Say hallo to Dad for me.

Barbara and Gavin kiss across John

Barbara OK. (*Into the phone*) Yes, I'm with you.
John (*into the mobile*) Is — Gavin — there?!
Barbara (*into the phone*) Yes.
John (*into the mobile*) Thank heavens! Put him on.

Barbara (*into the phone*) He's just about to leave actually. He sends his love. (*She waves goodbye to Gavin*)

Gavin exits by the Streatham front door

John (*into the mobile*) What?! No! Grab him. Stop him! I want to talk to him *now*.

Barbara crosses John and sits in the chair DR

Barbara (*into the phone*) I think he's made a date, actually. You'll laugh when I tell you!
John (*into the mobile*) Barbara!
Barbara (*into the phone*) Do you know how many Smiths there are in the London area?
John (*into the mobile*) Yes, not enough! Get Gavin!
Barbara (*into the phone*) Well, he's going round to see this Vicki Smith whose father is also called John Leonard and drives a taxi!
John (*into the mobile*) Please — get — Gavin!
Barbara (*into the phone*) Won't it keep until tonight?
John (*into the mobile; frantically*) Just get — Ga —— !

Mary storms in from the kitchen, carrying a glass of water and a bottle of aspirins

John stops in mid-shout

Mary (*over her shoulder; off*) That's the unfunniest joke I've ever heard!

Stanley enters awkwardly

Stanley It's the only one I know, actually.
Mary (*turning*) John ——
Barbara (*into the phone*) John!
Mary (*to John*) Are you talking?
Barbara (*into the phone*) John, have you gone into a tunnel again?
John (*to Mary*) I'm holding on for someone. One of my account customers. (*To Stanley*) Stanley! Car keys! (*To Mary*) Taxi's got a puncture.
Stanley I don't know where I could —— (*He feels in his pockets*)
Mary (*to Stanley*) Have you told John your stupid joke?
Stanley I don't think I have, no.
Barbara (*into the phone*) John, if you can hear me, I'll hang on until you're out of the tunnel.
John (*to Stanley*) Hurry up!
Mary (*to Stanley*) Go on. Tell him your joke.
John I don't want to hear it, Mary!

Mary (*to Stanley*) Just tell him!

Mary pulls Stanley across her and pushes him to John

Stanley A man goes to the vet. The vet says, "Open your mouth and say, 'Ahhh.'" The man says, "Why?" The vet says, "Your dog's just died."

John and Mary look totally blank. Stanley looks from John to Mary

(*Stressing the point*) A man goes to the vet ——

John and Mary still look blank

It's the only one I know.

Mary holds out the aspirins

Mary John, take these aspirins to Vicki. Make it up with her.
John No! (*To Stanley*) Stanley!
Stanley I can't think what I could have done with them! Oh, yes I do! I put them in one of my shopping bags for safety.
John God!

During the following, Stanley sits on the settee and empties out the contents of his shopping bags

Barbara (*into the phone*; *impatiently*) John, I don't know if you can hear me but I'm going to hang up.

Barbara rises

John (*into the mobile*) No! I'm still here.
Barbara (*into the phone*) Good, shall I see if I can catch Gavin and give him a message?
John (*into the mobile*) Yes, I think that would be the most practical arrangement. Tell him to stay exactly where he is. Not to move. (*To Mary*) I've got to pick up this old age pensioner from Tesco's. (*Into the mobile*) Tell him not to go anywhere until I arrive.
Barbara (*into the phone*) Won't be a second then. (*Still holding the cordless phone, she starts to move towards the front door*)
Mary (*to John*) Take these to Vicki. Tell her she can just see this Gavin boy for five minutes.
John No.

Mary All right! (*She moves towards the second bedroom*)

Gavin's motorbike is heard starting up. Barbara stops in the doorway

Barbara (*into the phone*) Hang on. I think I heard Gavin's motorbike starting up.
John (*into the mobile*) No!

Mary stops

Mary (*turning*) All right, I heard you.

   Mary exits into the second bedroom

John rushes above the settee to UR

John (*shouting after Mary*) She's not to leave her room! (*Into the mobile*) Barbara! Stop him. Don't talk. Just go and stop him. I'll be there in three minutes.
Barbara (*into the phone; with surprise*) From the Blackwall Tunnel?
John (*into the mobile*) Say five minutes. (*He switches off his mobile*)

   Barbara exits through the Streatham front door

John hurries to Stanley who is now surrounded by his holiday items

  For God's sake, Stanley!
Stanley I know they're here somewhere. (*He holds up a rubber bathing cap*) Bathing cap to protect my head from the sun.

John pulls Stanley up

John Never mind your bathing cap. I need your car. Let *me* look! (*He thrusts his mobile at Stanley to hold, pushes him* DLC *and starts madly searching through the holiday items; while searching*) And remember. Don't move till I get back.
Stanley I'm not happy about this, you know. If I'm late for Dad it'll totally confuse him.
John Never mind your dad!
Stanley He's confused enough as it is.
John Stanley! My life is at stake here!
Stanley I want to get to Felixstowe before it's dark.
John (*finding the car keys*) These them?

John rises and moves to Stanley

Stanley Yes. Look, I'm not up to all this.
John Course you are. (*He pats Stanley's cheek and moves to go*)
Stanley (*stopping him*) No, John. I'm not like you. I'm not good at all this
    subterfuge stuff. I mean, you know when I was trying to keep Mary in the
    kitchen. That terrible vet joke.
John Bloody funny, "Your dog's just died." I've got to go!

Stanley snatches the car keys

Stanley No! John! I'm sorry! I can't. I'm just the lodger, you know!
John (*suddenly serious*) No, you're not just the lodger, Stanley. You're my
    best friend. My very best friend. For twenty years. Before Vicki was born.
    You're the only person in the world I could have trusted with this awesome
    secret of mine. Yes! (*Getting emotional*) And you helped me out once
    before, didn't you? All those years ago. When I was nearly found out. You
    saved my marriages. You saved my life.
Stanley (*quite overcome*) I suppose I did, John, yes.

John snatches the car keys back

John Then stop arguing and save it again!

John hurries to the front door

Stanley John —— !

*John runs out of the front door, not realizing that he's left Stanley holding
his mobile*

*Stanley sighs, surveys his holiday items on the floor and goes to collect them.
He then realizes that he's holding John's mobile and runs to the door*

John! John! Your mobile.

*John, in Stanley's car, is heard pulling away with a screech of tyres. Stanley
slams the door and puts the mobile in his pocket*

Nice way to start a holiday!

*Stanley starts to pick up his holiday items and discovers the mask, snorkel and
bathing hat. He puts the mask on and, holding the snorkel and bathing hat,
he moves UL practising the breast stroke*

Barbara enters through the Streatham front door. She moves to Stanley's
R *dialling a number on her cordless phone*

*Stanley is swimming beside her practising the breast stroke. The mobile in
Stanley's pocket rings its tune. Stanley listens for a second, not knowing
where the music is coming from. He realizes and takes the mobile out of his
pocket*

(*Into the mobile*) Hallo!

*Stanley realizes he's wearing his mask and he takes it off, throwing the mask,
snorkel and hat behind the armchair* DLC

(*Into the mobile; nervously*) Hallo?
Barbara (*into the phone*) Oh, I thought I dialled 077 686 251.
Stanley (*nervously, into the mobile*) Oh, yes?
Barbara (*into the phone*) Is that my husband's mobile?
Stanley Ooo! (*He removes the mobile from his ear, looks at it in horror and
    returns it to his ear*)
Barbara (*into the phone*) Hallo?
Stanley (*into the mobile*) Hallo?
Barbara (*into the phone*) Is that Mr Smith's phone?
Stanley (*into the mobile*) Er — yes.
Barbara (*into the phone*) Can I speak to him, please?
Stanley (*into the mobile*) Er — no,
Barbara (*into the phone*) Who am I talking to?
Stanley (*into the mobile*) Er — me.
Barbara (*into the phone*) And who's that?

Stanley, eyeing the kitchen, moves DLC *to the settee*

Stanley (*into the mobile*) This is Mr Smith's answering service. We're trying
    to make it more personal, madam.
Barbara (*into the phone*) I was speaking to him just now.
Stanley (*into the mobile*) Yes but he's not taking calls at the moment,
    madam. Would you like to leave a message, madam?

Barbara moves DLC *talking*

Barbara (*into the phone*) Well, I'll be seeing him in a minute but I'll leave
    a message in case he checks in.
Stanley (*into the mobile*) What's the message, madam? It will be delivered
    to Mr Smith personally, madam.

Barbara (*into the phone*) Would you tell him that his wife called ——
Stanley (*into the mobile*) Mrs Smith called ——
Barbara (*into the phone*) And that I missed our son because he'd already left for Wimbledon.

Barbara walks in front of Stanley to DRC

Stanley (*into the mobile*) Already left for —— (*Realizing*) Bloody hell!

Barbara stops in surprise

Barbara (*into the phone*) What is it? What's happened?
Stanley (*into the mobile*) Little problem in the office here. One of the operators knocked a cup of coffee into my lap. (*Calling out*) You clumsy oaf, Sharon! (*In a high-pitched voice*) I'm sorry, Mr Wilkinson. I don't know what came over me. (*In a normal voice*) Get on with your work, Sharon! (*In a high-pitched voice*) Would you like another cup? (*In a normal voice*) No! (*In a high-pitched voice*) Whatever you say, Mr Wilkinson. (*In a normal voice*) Sharon!

Barbara is listening, bemused

(*Into the mobile*) Sorry about that. Sharon's new at Vodafone. Now are you absolutely positive you can't stop Gavin coming over to Wimbledon?
Barbara (*into the phone*) I told you, he's already —— (*Realizing*) How do you know his name's Gavin?

Stanley thinks for a moment

Stanley (*into the mobile*) All Mr Smith's personal details are on our computer, madam. And this telephone conversation may be recorded for your own protection, madam. Good-afternoon, madam. Have a nice day, madam. Thank you for using Vodafone Personal Answering Services, madam. (*He switches the mobile off*)

Barbara, perplexed, replaces her phone on its base

(*To himself, in anguish*) Oh, my God! Gavin!

Barbara hurries into the main bedroom

Stanley puts the mobile into his pocket, tiptoes ULC *to the front door and peers out*

Mary comes out of the second bedroom carrying an empty glass. She stops on seeing Stanley

Mary You still here?!
Stanley Ahh! (*He accidentally bangs the front door on his head*) Ah! Yes! Just thought I'd take a look out of the front door. Checking on the weather. It's still there. Yep, all set for Felixstowe. (*He closes the door*)
Mary (*pointing to the shopping on the floor*) Is all this stuff yours?
Stanley Yes
Mary Well get rid of it, go upstairs and push off to Felixstowe.

Mary goes to collect one of the empty mugs from the table UL

Stanley Certainly. No problem! Go upstairs. Collect Dad from Clapham. Push off to Felixstowe. Life's good!

Stanley collects up the items from settee. NB. The mask, bathing hat and snorkel are still behind the armchair DLC

Mary Right!
Stanley Yes. Life's good. Can't wait to get going.

Mary waits for him to go. Stanley doesn't

Mary Well, clear off upstairs then.

Mary pushes him out of the way and moves to get the other mug from the table behind the settee. Stanley looks anxiously towards the front door. Mary turns

Stanley Yes. Upstairs. To my flat. Where I live. The good life! You carry on then.
Mary Stanley!
Stanley Mary?
Mary If you don't clear off I shall kick you very hard where it hurts most.
Stanley Point taken.

Stanley rushes upstairs. Mary emits an angry sigh and exits into kitchen. Stanley's head appears around the banister. He checks that the coast is clear, then hurries downstairs. He hurries over to kitchen door and listens. He then tiptoes to the front door and opens it to look out. Gavin is standing in the doorway, wearing his crash helmet and about to ring the bell

Ahh!

Gavin steps in, removing his helmet

Gavin Hi, I'm Gavin!
Stanley (*looking to the kitchen*) Ooh!
Gavin Vicki's expecting me.
Stanley Yes. She can't see you and don't come back.

Stanley tries to close the door, but Gavin walks past him into the room

Gavin Hang on. She said to come over. I'm *Gavin*.
Stanley Goodbye, Gavin.
Gavin Gavin *Smith*. She invited me round for tea.
Stanley We've finished tea. Goodbye, Gavin!

Stanley takes Gavin's arm

Gavin Hold it. Can't I see Vicki?
Stanley Absolutely out of the question. Lovely meeting you, Gavin, and
   don't forget not to come back.

Stanley pulls Gavin across him to the door

Gavin Wait a minute. Are you her dad?

Stanley hesitates

Stanley I beg your pardon?
Gavin Are you Vicki's dad?
Stanley Vicki's dad.
Gavin Mr Smith.

Stanley considers this

Stanley Yes! Yes. Yes, I'm Mr Smith. The father of my daughter — er —
   Vicki's father. I'm the head of the —er — and I make the — er — I'm the
   big boss. The big Cappa de Chino. And Vicki can't see you.

Again Stanley tries to push Gavin. Gavin resists

Gavin But only half an hour ago she told me to come round.
Stanley That was half an hour ago, Gavin. The world has changed since then!
   Now, she can't see you. And she can't see you later. And she can't see you
   after that either. There's no future for you. It's all over. Goodbye, have a
   nice day!

Stanley pushes Gavin out

   Gavin exits

Stanley slams the door shut and leans against it, exhausted. The Wimbledon front doorbell rings. Stanley opens the door

   Gavin is standing there

   Bugger off!

Stanley slams the door and leans against it. The front doorbell goes again. Stanley looks mortified

   Mary enters from the kitchen. She is carrying a large saucepan. She stops on seeing Stanley

Stanley freezes with his back against the front door. He has a look of horror. He manages to turn his look to a happy contented smile

Mary Are you still here?
Stanley Sort of.
Mary That was the doorbell, wasn't it?
Stanley Sort of.
Mary Well, see who it is.

Mary moves to Stanley who grabs her and marches her DLC away from the front door

Stanley I know who it is. It's for me.
Mary For you?
Stanley Yes. It's my visitor.
Mary Visitor?
Stanley Yes. My visitor. For me. I've been expecting them — and now they've arrived. For a meeting. Very important. It's going to be a very *long* important meeting. Go on for hours. We mustn't be disturbed.

Stanley tries to push Mary towards the kitchen

Mary I thought you were leaving for Felixstowe.
Stanley That's been cancelled.
Mary What about your father?

Stanley He's been cancelled, too. I mean postponed. We're going later. After I've seen my visitor.

Mary Aren't you going to let them in?

Stanley No. Well — er — not while you're here. I need to be alone with my visitor.

Stanley tries to push Mary to the kitchen

Mary What the hell are you talking about?

Stanley That's a very fair question.

The doorbell goes again. Stanley looks aghast. He's beginning to crack!

Mary, please! I don't want you to see my visitor and I don't want my visitor to see you!

Mary Why on earth not?

Stanley Because it's private and personal!

Mary Private and ——

Stanley Personal! Very personal. Very private.

Mary Is this anything to do with your problem you were discussing with John?

Stanley Yes it is.

Mary Your emotional and sexual problem?

Stanley hesitates. The doorbell goes again

Stanley Yes! My emotional and — er ——

Mary Sexual.

Stanley — problem.

Mary And somebody's calling round in the middle of the afternoon to sort it out.

Stanley hesitates then nods his head

Well, I'd be grateful if you'd entertain the young lady upstairs!

Mary storms into the kitchen

Stanley closes his eyes and looks up to heaven in anguish. The doorbell goes again. Stanley is in turmoil. He rushes to the kitchen door and opens it

Stanley (*yelling into the kitchen*) Don't come in. This won't take long! (*He slams the kitchen door and starts to hurry to the front door, but stops. He* *returns to kitchen door and locks it*) Lock Mary. (*He starts for the front door but stops. He goes to the second bedroom door and locks it*) Lock Vicki. (*He then hurries up to front door and opens it; furiously*) Gavin ——— !

Gavin, very determinedly walks in and past him

Gavin Look, I'm sorry, Mr Smith.
Stanley So am I, Gavin! Now sod off to Streatham!

Stanley turns Gavin, but Gavin resists and walks further into the room to below the settee, followed by a frantic Stanley

But I really don't see why Vicki can't ———
Stanley Gavin!
Gavin No, I don't see why she can't see me!

Stanley grabs Gavin by the lapels and pulls him close

Stanley She can't see you — you horrible nasty pervert — because she can't see you! Understand, you computerized clot?! She can't see you! She *won't* see you! She's *unable* to see you!!
Gavin You mean there's something wrong with her eyesight.
Stanley (*yelling*) Yes! She's got no eyesight! Now go home!
Gavin (*with amazement*) No eyesight?
Stanley No bloody eyesight! It's bloody sad!
Gavin (*agog*) You mean she's blind?

Stanley desperately tries to calm himself

Stanley Vicki is visually impaired, Gavin. Too much television. Too much Internet. Started off as eye-strain and then suddenly — one morning: "Where's the breakfast table, Daddy?" Nothing.
Gavin That's terrible!
Stanley Yes. I knew you'd understand, Gavin. Goodbye — for ever.

Stanley turns Gavin gently. Gavin turns back

Gavin She must be pretty amazing.
Stanley Yes!
Gavin I mean if she can't see, how can she operate her computer like that?

Stanley considers this

Stanley It's programmed for voice recognition.
Gavin That's fantastic!

Stanley All on the National Health. Off you go, Gavin!

Stanley turns Gavin but Gavin breaks DLC

Gavin Hang on. Are you saying she won't see me because she's visually impaired?
Stanley (*grabbing Gavin*) That's right!
Gavin No, I mean I realize she *physically* wouldn't be able to see me — but are you saying she *won't* see me?
Stanley Yes, she won't see you!
Gavin Like she doesn't *want* to see me.
Stanley That's it!!
Gavin Why not?
Stanley (*yelling*) I've told you why!!!
Gavin No, you haven't. You've told me she's visually impaired and is *unable* to see me.

Stanley grabs Gavin's lapels

Stanley You're bloody argumentative, aren't you, Gavin?!
Gavin It just seems peculiar, Mr Smith. Vicki inviting me round and then you saying she won't see me because she's visually impaired.

Stanley is now almost weeping in desperation

Stanley It's not just because she's visually impaired. She suddenly realized that, at fifteen, she wasn't yet ready for that kind of deep meaningful relationship.
Gavin Deep, meaningful ...? We've been chatting on line, Mr Smith, that's all.

During the following Stanley moves a bemused Gavin towards the front door

Stanley But Vicki could see where it was leading to. So, very bravely, she has decided not to put you both through that emotional agony — and never to see you. Definitely. Final. No arguments. Goodbye. Stiff upper lip, Gav.

There is banging from the second bedroom door

Vicki (*off*) Hey, I'm locked in again!

Gavin looks to Stanley

Stanley (*calling sweetly*) Coming!

Stanley smiles at Gavin

   (*Sweetly*) Off you go, Gavin.

Stanley turns Gavin. There is more knocking. Gavin turns back

Vicki (*off*) Hey!
Stanley (*calling sweetly*) Won't be a moment!

Stanley smiles at Gavin and turns him around

Vicki (*off*) Is that you, Uncle Stanley?!

Gavin turns. Stanley smiles at him

Stanley (*to Gavin*) Uncle Stanley lives with us. (*Calling sweetly; in a silly voice*) No-oo!
Vicki (*off*) Hey!
Gavin (*to Stanley*) Is that your Vicki? (*He eagerly moves towards the bedroom*)

Stanley grabs Gavin and pulls him across

Stanley No! No, that's not Vicki. Vicki's somewhere else. That's Mrs Smith.
Gavin Mrs Smith?
Stanley Yes. My — er — my ——
Gavin Wife?
Stanley Thank you, Gavin, yes. Yes, that's my wife. That's my Mary.

There is more banging from Vicki

Vicki (*off*) Open this door!
Stanley Yes, I've had to lock her in as usual. She's a bit funny. She wasn't originally ... She wasn't funny when we first got married — but she went funny after Vicki lost her eyesight. The same day. It was quite a morning, I can tell you.
Gavin I'm sorry.
Stanley Thank you, Gavin.
Vicki (*off*) If somebody doesn't open this door, I'll kick it in!
Stanley (*to Gavin*) She gets violent, too.

Stanley turns Gavin to go as Mary bangs on the kitchen door

Mary (*off*) Hey!

Stanley and Gavin turn and look to the kitchen. Gavin looks to Stanley who smiles

(*Off*) Anybody there?!
Stanley (*to Gavin*) That's my wife's sister.
Gavin Is she locked in as well?

Gavin moves to the kitchen but Stanley grabs him

Stanley Oh, yes.
Gavin So, she's funny, too, is she?
Stanley Very!
Gavin Blimey.
Stanley Yes. That's — er — Rosie. Rosie went funny the same morning as Mary. You know, the day Vicki —— (*He mimes being unable to see*)
Gavin Cor!
Stanley Yes, Cor!

There is violent banging from Mary

Mary (*off*) Hey, the door's locked!
Stanley Rosie gets violent, too.
Mary (*off*) Are you still in there, Stanley?! Stanley!
Stanley Mary's sister, Rosie, is married to Stanley. And, as Rosie is Mary's sister — (*almost crying*) that's why Stanley is Vicki's uncle.
Gavin And Uncle Stanley and Auntie Rosie live here, too.
Stanley You have to look after the in-laws, don't you?

There is banging from the kitchen

Mary (*off*) Hey!

They look to the kitchen. There is banging from the second bedroom door

Vicki (*off*) Hey!

They look to the bedroom. Gavin looks at Stanley

Stanley (*desperately*) I think we could be in for a double whammy here.

Stanley tries to push Gavin but he resists

Gavin No, I really want to see Vicki. You've made her sound fantastic.

Stanley (*pleading*) I didn't mean to, Gavin!
Vicki (*off*) Hey!
Mary (*off*) Hey!

Mary and Vicki both bang their doors at the same time

Stanley Look, if Mary and Rosie are getting violent together, you'd better
   clear off.
Gavin They don't scare me.
Stanley They bloody scare *me*, Gavin!

Stanley tries to move him

Gavin No! I want to meet your Vicki!

*The two doors are banged by Mary and Vicki. Stanley is now beside himself
with confusion*

Stanley OK! OK! Wait upstairs in my flat.

Stanley turns Gavin, but Gavin stops

Gavin (*with surprise*) Your flat?

Stanley hesitates

Stanley Yes, I took the flat upstairs when Mary started getting violent. We
   eat together, but it's wiser to sleep apart. It's also a safe refuge for my
   brother-in-law, Stanley, when Rosie gets violent.
Gavin OK. And you'll tell Vicki where I am.
Stanley You might have a bit of a wait, Gav. She's been slightly delayed.
   Little accident. Fell off her bicycle.
Gavin (*with astonishment*) Her bicycle?

Stanley realizes what he's said

Stanley She has this computerized image of a bicycle — on her laptop. And
   because she has this voice recognition apparatus — it gives her exercise.
   But, like I say, she fell off — in her excitement. You wait in my flat! I'll
   send Vicki up.

Stanley turns Gavin, but Gavin turns back

Gavin How exactly does this computerized image of a bicycle work?

Stanley stares at Gavin for a moment

Stanley You must be a real pain in the arse in school, Gavin!

Stanley shoves Gavin upstairs

 Gavin exits

 Barbara, worried, enters and goes to the Streatham phone

As Barbara dials, Stanley tiptoes towards the kitchen and listens. There is a banging from the second bedroom. Stanley turns

Vicki (*off*) If you don't open this door, Dad, I'll break it down!

Stanley hesitates then hurriedly tiptoes towards the second bedroom. The mobile phone rings its tune

Stanley (*jumping*) Ahhh! (*He realizes it's the mobile, grabs it from his pocket and presses the on switch and listens*)
Barbara (*into the phone*) Hallo, John! Can you hear me? Where are you?

Stanley gives a few heavy breaths and switches the mobile off

 Ooh!

 Barbara storms off into the main bedroom

Vicki (*off*) Dad!
Mary (*off*) Stanley!
Vicki (*off*) Hey!

Stanley dithers between the two doors

 John hurries in through the Streatham front door. John is now minus his jacket and in shirt sleeves

Stanley quickly tiptoes across towards the second bedroom

John (*breathless, calling urgently*) Gavin ...! Barbara ...! Gavin ...! Barbara ...!

Stanley unlocks the bedroom

John exits into the main bedroom. Vicki angrily enters from the bedroom. She has showered, changed into something "groovy" and carries a shoulder bag

Vicki Now, listen, Dad —— !
Stanley Ssh!
Vicki Uncle Stan! What's going on? You said it wasn't you. (*She crosses in front of Stanley*) Where's Dad? Did you lock me in? Was that Gavin Smith at the front door?
Stanley One question at a time, please! Your father's picking up an old age pensioner from Tesco's, yes, it *was* Gavin Smith at the front door, and yes, I did lock you in.

Mary bangs on the kitchen door

Mary (*off*) Hey!
Stanley (*to Vicki*) I locked your mother in, too!
Vicki Why for God's sake?
Stanley (*crying*) I can't remember! (*He sits in armchair* DRC)

Vicki unlocks the kitchen door

  Mary storms in

Mary (*as she enters*) Now, what's going ...?! (*With surprise*) Vicki! Did you lock that kitchen door?
Vicki No, Uncle Stan did.
Mary Why?
Vicki He can't remember.

Mary crosses to Stanley

Mary (*angrily*) Did you lock that kitchen door?

Stanley nods

  Why?!
Stanley It seemed like a good idea at the time.
Mary Silly sod. (*Coldly*) And where's your visitor?!
Stanley Upstairs.
Mary So what are you doing down here?
Stanley God only knows.
Vicki Never mind his visitor. Where's Gavin?

Stanley quickly rises

Stanley Gavin's gone!
Mary I didn't even know he'd arrived.
Stanley And he's not coming back!
Vicki What? Why?
Stanley I sent him packing.
Vicki Packing?
Mary (*to Stanley*) What's it got to do with you?
Stanley (*quickly sitting*) Nothing.
Vicki Right! I'm going round to Gavin's house.
Stanley (*rises*) No!
Mary You keep out of this, Stanley!

Stanley sits

Vicki He gave me the address. 47 Lewin Road, Streatham.

Vicki exits by the front door

Stanley (*rising*) No, you mustn't!
Mary Shut up!

Stanley sits

Vicki returns pushing a bicycle

Vicki I'm going to borrow your bike, Mum? Is that OK?

During the next three lines Vicki goes to cupboard UL *and gets her crash helmet*

Mary Yes, but I'm not sure you should go without Dad's permission.
Stanley (*standing up*) Quite right!

Mary turns angrily to Stanley. He sits

Vicki Dad's being totally unreasonable. And you're a traitor, Uncle Stan!

Vicki exits by the front door with her bicycle, still clutching her shoulder bag

Mary (*calling after Vicki*) Well, be back in time for supper. I'm making us a lamb stew! (*She slams the door closed*)

Stanley (*rising*) Oh, my God!
Mary (*to Stanley*) This is all your fault.
Stanley (*sitting*) I thought it must be.
Mary When did Gavin arrive?
Stanley Just now.
Mary While your "personal and private" visitor was upstairs?
Stanley Er — yes.
Mary Well, I suggest you get back and let her finish off your treatment.

Mary goes into the kitchen

Stanley rises and moves URC, *towards the Wimbledon front door*

Stanley (*to himself*) I must warn John about Vicki. (*He takes out the mobile and looks at the key-pad; to himself*) Re-dial. Re-dial. Where are you?

In Streatham, John enters from the main bedroom followed by Barbara, who shuts the bedroom door

John (*as he enters*) You should have stopped him!
Barbara Gavin says she sounds a very nice girl!
John She's a horrible little tart!
Barbara You don't know what she's like.
John Yes, I do! (*Quickly*) No, I don't. That's not the point. I told you to keep him here.

John heads for the Streatham front door followed by Barbara

Stanley Where the hell is it?
Barbara Johnny! Where are you going?
Stanley Ah! (*He finds the re-dial button and presses it*)
John I suddenly remembered. I've left this old age pensioner standing outside Tesco's.
Barbara Well, don't forget, I've booked us into this new vegetarian restaurant.
John Yeah, I might have to join you there. If I'm late order me liver and bacon.

John hurries out of the front door

Barbara goes to follow as the Streatham phone rings. She lifts the receiver

Barbara (*into the phone*) Hallo?

Stanley (*into the mobile; nervously*) Is that Mrs Smith?

Barbara (*into the phone*) Yes.

Stanley (*into the mobile*) Ah — well, I need to speak to Mr Smith please! It's urgent!

Barbara (*into the phone*) Who's this?

Stanley moves to DR, *eyeing the kitchen*

Stanley (*into the mobile*) Mr Smith's personal answering service. I have a very important message for him.

Barbara (*into the phone*) He's just left.

Stanley (*into the mobile*) What?!

Barbara (*into the phone*) He came in and rushed straight out again.

Stanley (*into the mobile*) Bloody hell!

Barbara moves RC *startled*

Barbara (*into the phone*) What is it? What's happened?

Stanley (*calling out for Barbara's benefit*) You clumsy oaf, Sharon! (*In a high-pitched voice*) I'm sorry, Mr Wilkinson, I'm having one of those days. (*In a normal voice*) Do it again and you're fired. (*In a high-pitched voice*) But, Mr Wilkinson — (*In a normal voice*) Sharon ... ! (*Into the mobile*) Look, I've got to get hold of Mr Smith right away!

Barbara (*into the phone*) Well, ring him on his mobile.

Stanley (*into the mobile*) Good thinking —— ! (*He takes the mobile from his ear, goes to dial then he realizes. Into the mobile; panicking*) Look, I don't think you ought to stay in the house.

Barbara (*into the phone*) What?

Stanley (*into the mobile*) You should go out for the rest of the day!

Barbara (*into the phone; bemused*) I beg your pardon?

Stanley (*into the mobile*) In case somebody —anybody — calls. Just get out of the house. Now!

Barbara (*into the phone*) I don't know what you're talking about.

Stanley crosses below the settee to DLC, *talking*

Stanley (*into the mobile*) That makes two of us. Please! Just go. Now!

Barbara (*into the phone*) Why?!

Stanley (*into the mobile; gabbling*) It's a special "dining-out" offer from Vodafone ... Any restaurant you like absolutely free. Eat as much as you want, Vodafone pays — wine included. But you have to be seated for dinner by — (*he looks at his watch*) 4:45 p.m.; you've nearly missed it. Hurry!

Barbara (*into the phone*) Hang on a second. Does this offer include that new
vegetarian restaurant in Streatham, High Road?
Stanley It includes the *Savoy*, the *Ivy* and *Harrods*. Hurry!!

*Mary, unseen by Stanley enters from the kitchen with a pile of plates and
cutlery. She is heading for the dining-room but stops on seeing Stanley.
During the following she moves towards him*

(*Into the mobile*) It's a fantastic offer!
Barbara (*into the phone; confused*) All right! All right! I'll think about it.
Stanley (*into the mobile*) No, don't think about it, do it! Drop everything and
go. Do it now! (*He turns and sees Mary. He backs away from Mary while
speaking to* DRC; *into the mobile*) Yes — er — do it. Now. Just go. Don't
wait. Get out of the house. Lock the door and go. (*He switches off the
mobile*)

Barbara, bemused, looks at her phone and hurries into the main bedroom

(*To Mary*) Just checking that Dad's set his burglar alarm.
Mary You don't seem very anxious to get back to your visitor.
Stanley Oh, I am.

Mary moves to Stanley and pushes him URC *to behind the settee*

Mary Well, I'm anxious to get on with preparing supper for me and Vicki
so — have a nice time upstairs and have a nice time in Felixstowe.
Stanley Thank you. I'll get back to the flat and finish — er — say, "thank
you and goodbye"——

Gavin enters from upstairs

Gavin Excuse me ———

*Stanley closes his eyes in anguish. Mary's initial look of surprise turns to
indignation as she realizes that Stanley's "visitor" is a young man. She backs
away and sits on the back of the armchair* DRC

Stanley (*to Gavin; politely*) I'll be with you in just a moment.

Gavin comes downstairs

Gavin I thought you might have forgotten about me.

Stanley grabs Gavin's arm, desperately attempting to be nonchalant

Stanley (*to Gavin*) No, it's all in hand ... ! I mean, I'm just coming … ! I'll be up in a… ! Just go back upstairs!!

Gavin moves DLC

Gavin (*to Mary; pleasantly*) Are you Mrs Smith?

Mary moves DRC

Mary (*coldly*) Yes, I *am* Mrs Smith!

Stanley quickly moves to Gavin

Stanley (*brightly*) Yes, she's Mrs Smith. (*Cosily*) This is Mary.
Gavin Oh. Not Rosie then.

Stanley crosses to Mary

Stanley No, not "rosy". (*He pats Mary's cheek*) Yes, looking a little bit pale, Mary.

Mary slaps Stanley's hand and Stanley sits on the R *arm of the settee*

Gavin (*moving to Mary*) How do you do. (*He holds out his hand*)

Mary just looks at him sternly

Mary (*coldly*) How do you do.
Gavin (*to Mary*) Oh, I haven't introduced myself ——
Stanley (*rising*) You don't have to introduce yourself!
Mary No, you don't!
Gavin Oh. Well, in case you're worried, Mum said it would be all right for me to come over.
Mary (*with amazement*) Your mother?
Gavin Yeah.
Mary Your mother *approves*?
Gavin Yeah. Dad doesn't know yet but he won't mind either.
Stanley Lovely! (*To Gavin*) I think you can go back upstairs now.

Stanley takes Gavin's elbow but Gavin doesn't move

Gavin (*to Mary*) Hey, wasn't it funny the two of us meeting the way we did?
Mary (*coldly*) I really wouldn't know.
Stanley (*brightly*) She really wouldn't know!

Stanley takes Gavin's elbow but Gavin doesn't move

Gavin On the Internet.
Mary (*coldly*) I see!
Stanley (*to Gavin*) Back upstairs.

Stanley grabs Gavin's hand to pull him away

Gavin I mean, when you think there's over a hundred thousand of us in the London area alone.
Mary Oh! (*She looks at them holding hands and storms off towards the kitchen, stops and turns*) Oh! (*She opens the kitchen door, but turns back*) Ohh!

Mary exits into the kitchen

Gavin crosses Stanley, looking after Mary

Gavin (*to Stanley*) You're right. She *is* funny.
Stanley Yes!
Gavin She looked as though she might be getting violent again.
Stanley Definitely.
Gavin So the pair of them are in there, are they?
Stanley (*blankly*) Pair of them?
Gavin Your wife and Auntie Rosie. They might kill each other.
Stanley Ah, no. We keep them apart. At tea-time we lock Auntie Rosie in the attic. I'll show you to the front door. (*He goes to move Gavin*)
Gavin Hang on. You said you were getting Vicki.
Stanley Did I say that?
Gavin Yes.
Stanley (*suddenly*) Oh! Hell! I forgot to give you the *message*.
Gavin What message?
Stanley From Vicki. Put it right out of my mind having to deal with Mary in the kitchen and Rosie in the attic. Vicki's waiting for you in Poppy's Tea Rooms.

Satnley makes to move Gavin but Gavin stops

Gavin (*with surprise*) Where?
Stanley Little café in the High Street. She thought it best for you not to meet here with her mother being funny and violent, potty Auntie Rosie on the loose as well, so Vicki's waiting for you at Poppy's Tea Rooms.

Stanley goes to move Gavin but Gavin stops

Gavin Where's that then?
Stanley Turn left out of the house, down Kenilworth Avenue to the High Street. Turn right and Poppy's Tea rooms is about six hundred yards on the left. You got that?

During the next two lines, John rushes in through the Wimbledon front door and stops dead in horror at seeing Stanley standing there with Gavin

Gavin I think so. Left, right and left.
Stanley You've got it. Vicki's expecting you.

Stanley turns Gavin towards the front door and John . John dives head-first over the settee and buries his head in the cushions. Gavin is stopped in his tracks by the sight of the flying figure. Stanley is mortified but quickly takes the anorak from behind the settee, covers John and tucks him in

Stanley (*pointing to John*) That's my brother-in-law, Mr Gardner. Stanley's popped down for his afternoon nap. He needs all the sleep he can get with a wife like Rosie.
Gavin Right. (*To the recumbent John*) How do you do, Mr Gardner.

John emits a loud snore

Stanley Off you pop to Poppy's, Gavin. Left, right, left.
Gavin Right. Will Vicki have got to Poppy's Tea Rooms all by herself?
Stanley Yes, yes, yes!
Gavin I suppose she's got a guide dog as well as a white stick, has she?
Stanley Definitely. (*He pushes Gavin out of the front door*)

Gavin exits

John, bemused, emerges from the anorak, as Stanley staggers DRC and collapses in the armchair

John White stick and a guide dog?!
Stanley You don't know what I've been through!

John rises

John And what's all that about me being your brother-in-law?

Stanley That's right. I'm you, you're me, your daughter's blind and Mary's mad!

John What?

Stanley And wait till you meet potty Auntie Rosie in the attic!!

John Potty Auntie Rosie in the —— ?!

Stanley Oh, yes, and Mary thinks I'm having it off with your son!!!

John Having it off with my ... ?!!

Stanley (*rising*) The main thing is I've kept Gavin and Vicki apart.

John's fury turns to delight

John Oh, that's brilliant, Stanley!

Stanley I've sent Gavin down to Poppy's Tea Rooms to meet Vicki.

John Oh, that's ... ! (*Realizing; with horror*) You've done what?!

Stanley It's all right. Vicki's not there.

John (*realizing*) Oh, clever, Stanley!

Stanley She's gone round to your house in Streatham.

John Oh, clever ... ! (*Realizing*) She's gone where?

Stanley I couldn't stop her.

John (*mortified*) She'll meet Barbara! I've got to get back there right away.
  (*He thrusts the anorak on to Stanley and moves*)

Stanley grabs him

Stanley John —— !

John Hold the fort, Stanley!

Stanley No, I can't cope any more!

John I've got to go. My two families are at stake.

Stanley What about *my* family! Auntie Rosie, Uncle Stanley, crazy Mary ——

John Stanley! Every second counts!

John moves to below the L end of the settee. Stanley grabs him

Stanley No, I need my car. Dad's waiting for me to pick him up in Clapham. We're going on holiday!

John Take a taxi!

Stanley All the way to Felixstowe?! Give me my car keys!

John I've got to go!!

Behind John, Gavin hurries through the front door

Gavin (*referring to Stanley*) Mr Smith! I couldn't quite remember —— (*He stops*)

John turns and dives headlong over the front of the armchair DLC. His head hangs over the back out of view with his knees on the seat and his bottom in the air

During the following, John, out of view of the audience, puts on the mask, the snorkel and the bathing hat. Gavin walks down to the L side of the armchair to view the spectacle. Stanley hurries down to the R side of the armchair. He drapes the anorak over John

Stanley Uncle Stanley's been sleep-walking. What are you doing back here, Gavin?
Gavin Well, I couldn't quite remember whether you said Poppy's Tea Rooms was left, right and left or right ... (*Referring to John's bottom*) He might topple over, mightn't he?
Stanley No, he sleeps like that all the time. It's left, right, left.
Gavin I really think he'd be more comfortable on the settee.

Gavin gets hold of John's arm and pulls him up and round. Stanley grabs John's other arm. They all struggle

Stanley No!
Gavin I can manage!
Stanley No! He mustn't be disturbed! Gavin!

Finally, John is propelled round facing front. Gavin backs away DR in amazement at John standing there, in an anorak, wearing a mask, a snorkel and a bathing hat. For a moment, John is at a loss. He then bows politely and does a breaststroke towards the front door. As he gets to the door, the doorbell gives a long urgent ring. He stops for a moment and then continues on past the front door — this time swimming a fast crawl. He swims the crawl DRC, in front of the settee towards the kitchen. He reaches the kitchen

Mary enters wearing kitchen gloves and carrying a dish of steaming vegetables

Stanley is now masked by the open kitchen door

Mary (*as she enters*) Stanley, will you answer that —— !

Mary stops in amazement at the sight of John, who has come to a halt in front of her swimming the crawl. John hesitates for a fraction of a second and then moves backwards swimming the backstroke. He stops in front of the settee. The doorbell rings. John quickly looks to the front door, then to Mary and then to Gavin. He holds his nose, jumps and sinks into the "water"

Music

Black-out

CURTAIN

ACT II

The same. The action is continuous

When the CURTAIN *rises, the doorbell is ringing urgently and then stops. Mary moves to John below the settee*

Mary (*to John*) What the hell are you doing?
John (*in a muffled voice through the mouthpiece*) Giving swimming lessons.

John mimes the breaststroke

Mary (*not understanding*) What?
John (*muffled*) Giving swimming lessons.

John mimes the breaststroke. Stanley appears from behind the kitchen door

Stanley (*interrupting; with a nasal voice*) He's giving me swimming lessons.

Stanley mimes the breaststroke

John (*muffled voice*) I have to get back on the road. (*He mimes driving a car*)
Mary (*not understanding*) What?
Stanley (*with a nasal voice*) He says he has to get back on the road. (*He mimes driving a car*)
John (*to Mary; in a muffled voice*) I'll go the back way. Through the kitchen. (*He indicates through the kitchen*)
Stanley (*with a nasal voice*) He says he'll go the back way through ——
Mary (*interrupting*) Shut up, Stanley!
John (*in a muffled voice*) So, don't forget! Breaststroke. (*He mimes a vigorous breast stroke*) Crawl. (*He mimes a vigorous crawl*) Backstroke. (*He mimes a vigorous backstroke*) And butterfly.

John "butterflies" through the kitchen door and exits

Stanley (*calling after John*) Thank you! (*To Mary*) I must remember that. (*In a nasal voice*) Breaststroke, crawl ——

Mary hits Stanley's arm

Mary Shut up! (*Referring to Gavin*) And why do I keep finding him here?
Stanley Just lucky, I suppose.

There is the sound of the car noisily starting up and John screeching away at frantic speed. Mary crosses Stanley to the kitchen door

Mary (*slamming the door*) He'll kill himself!
Stanley That would solve all our problems.

The doorbell rings again — now very urgently

Mary (*moving to Stanley*) Haven't you opened that door, yet?
Stanley (*apprehensively*) We don't know who it might be.

Gavin moves to below the settee

Gavin Hey, it might be Vicki!
Stanley (*anxiously*) No, she's gone round … (*He stops; foolishly*) Round. Round. Round and round the garden ——
Mary (*hitting Stanley*) Shut up! (*Referring to Gavin*) What's he got to do with our Vicki?
Stanley (*gabbling*) I was telling him about her. (*To Gavin*) Wasn't I? Telling you about her. What a delightful girl she is. Sweet child. Lovely nature.
Gavin But a dreadful thing about her eye ——
Stanley (*frantically interrupting*) Her eye — ! Her eye — ! Her IQ! Her IQ! is not good — but she's working on it, isn't she, Mary?
Mary You two leave my daughter out of your conversation if you don't mind.
Stanley That's a very good idea!

The doorbell goes again

Yes, I think I *will* open the door. Safer. (*He opens the front door*)

Stanley's Dad is standing there clutching a suitcase and his heavy-duty metal stick. Dad is in his eighties and fluctuates between senilty, alertness and cussedness

Dad (*to Stanley*) I've been waiting for you in Clapham!

There is a momentary pause and then Stanley slams the door in his face. Mary is amazed at Stanley's action

Mary That was your father.
Stanley I know!
Mary You slammed the door in his face!
Stanley It's not raining.
Mary Yes! You'd be ashamed if your dad saw you with him! (*She points to Gavin*)
Stanley Definitely!
Gavin (*with surprise*) Me?

The doorbell goes again. Stanley pulls Gavin across him to the kitchen

Stanley (*to Gavin*) Don't forget it's left, right, left. Go this way! (*He indicates the open kitchen door*)
Mary (*to Gavin*) And don't come back!
Gavin I'll try not to!

Gavin hurries out through the kitchen

Stanley Sweet boy. He's popping into Poppy's for a coffee on his way home.
Mary I'm absolutely shattered, Stanley.
Stanley It's been a long day for you, Mary.
Mary About you! I mean, I don't care whether you're macho, homo or ambidextrous ——
Stanley Very politically correct, Mary.
Mary But, for heaven's sake, that boy is only about sixteen years old.
Stanley No, no, I think he's nearer seventeen, Mary, if you look. Bit of a beard, starting on ——
Mary (*interrupting*) Stanley! I just don't want any more of that sort of thing in this house, do you understand?
Stanley Of course.

The doorbell rings again

Mary You'd better let your father in.
Stanley Thank you.
Mary Does your poor old dad know what you get up to?
Stanley God, I hope not.

Mary gives Stanley a glare and exits into the kitchen

Stanley takes a deep breath and opens the front door

Dad, very irate, is still there, clutching his suitcase and his walking stick. He is about to speak

Not a word!

Stanley grabs Dad's arm and unceremoniously pulls him into the room. Dad, angry, goes to speak

Not a word!

Stanley grabs Dad's suitcase. Dad, angry, goes to speak

Not a word! (*He pushes the door to, so that it's not completely shut*) This has been the worst day of my life!

Stanley pulls Dad across him to the stairs. Dad turns and goes to speak

Not a word! Don't ask me why I didn't collect you. Don't ask me why we're late. Don't ask me what time we'll get to Felixstowe and don't ask me where the car is because I've lent the car to the most annoying, conniving, obnoxious man in the world!

Dad goes to speak

Not a word! I'm taking you upstairs, sitting you in front of the television and you're watching *Coronation Street* until my life is re-assembled.

Dad goes to speak

Not a word, you old bat!

Stanley pushes Dad up the stairs and they exit

After a moment the Streatham front door bursts open

John, shattered and totally out of breath, rushes in. He is no longer wearing his anorak. He stands in the doorway gasping for breath. He goes to yell for Barbara but only panted breath emerges. He tries again; same result

John (*finally*) Barbara —— ! (*He hurries to the kitchen, leaving the front door open. He opens the kitchen door; hoarsely*) Barbara!

John exits into the kitchen, closing the door. Barbara enters from the main bedroom

Barbara (*as she enters*) Is that you, Johnny? (*She moves to the dining-room. Opening the door*) Johnny?

Barbara exits into the dining-room, closing the door. John comes out of the kitchen, slams the door and hurries to the main bedroom

John (*opening the door*) Barbara!

John exits into the main bedroom, closing the door. Barbara enters from the dining-room, slams the door and moves to the kitchen

Barbara (*opening the door*) Johnny?

Barbara exits into the kitchen, closing the door. John comes out of the main bedroom, slams door and hurries to the dining-room

John (*opening the door*) Barbara!

John exits into the dining-room, closing the door. Vicki appears in the open doorway, carrying her shoulder bag and pushing her bike

Vicki Hallo? (*She moves* DRC) Hallo? (*She rests her bike in the doorway, removes her helmet and walks in*)

Barbara enters from the kitchen

Barbara (*as she enters*) Johnny —— ?
Vicki (*jumping*) Oh!
Barbara Where did you come from?
Vicki Wimbledon. I'm sorry. The door was open. I'm Vicki Smith.

Barbara hurries to Vicki

Barbara Oh! Lovely! I thought Gavin had gone round to see *you*. (*She takes Vicki's helmet and puts it on the table behind the settee*)

John, unseen by Barbara and Vicki, appears in the dining-room doorway and freezes

Vicki Well, there was a sort of a misunderstanding. My dad's a bit of a moron.

John reacts and silently retreats into the dining-room leaving the door ajar slightly

Barbara Come and sit down. Are you all right for time?

Barbara sits Vicki in the chair DLC

Vicki Well, I wouldn't mind waiting actually. I think Gavin might be back in a minute.

Barbara moves to the kitchen

Barbara Lovely. Cup of tea?
Vicki Have you got a Coke?
Barbara I've got a homemade raspberry and carrot juice!
Vicki (*trying to be polite*) Never had one of those.
Barbara And I want to hear all about your dad.

Barbara opens the kitchen door

Vicki I want to hear all about Gavin's dad, too. Is Mr Smith around?
Barbara Well, I thought he was but he must have rushed out again. He never stops. Got enough energy for two people.
Vicki Yeah. Sounds just like *my* dad.

Barbara exits. John appears in the dining-room doorway as Barbara immediately returns hitting, but also masking John, with the door

Barbara (*to Vicki*) Won't be a sec then.

Barbara exits into the kitchen

John immediately steps down

John Quick!
Vicki (*jumping*) Ahh! (*With amazement*) Dad!
John (*lifting her*) Come on.
Vicki What the —— !? Where the hell did you come from?
John Never mind. You've got to go home.

John pushes Vicki below the settee

Vicki I'm having a raspberry and carrot juice with Mrs Smith and I'm waiting for Gavin. (*She sits on the settee*)

John lifts her

John Vicki, you don't understand! Please I beg you! You've got to go home!

John pushes Vicki R. She stops

Vicki (*obstinately*) Why?!

John hesitates for a brief moment

John Uncle Stanley's died.

Vicki tries to assimilate this

Vicki (*blankly*) What?
John Uncle Stanley — he's dead. He's calling for you. (*Realizing*) I mean he's very nearly dead. And he's calling for you. Shocking accident.

Vicki collapses in an armchair DRC

Vicki (*shattered*) Uncle Stanley?
John Yes.
Vicki I can't believe it!

John lifts Vicki. She inadvertently leaves her shoulder bag in the chair

John Neither can I. (*To Vicki*) He wants you. I don't think there's much time.
Vicki What happened?
John He fell off the roof.
Vicki The roof?!
John Just get home as fast as you can.

John pushes Vicki up to the door but she hurriedly moves to the kitchen

Vicki Hang on, I'd better explain to Mrs Smith.
John No! Just get on your bike and go.

John turns to Vicki to push her out

   Barbara enters from the kitchen with a glass of juice

Barbara One raspberry and ... Oh! It *was* you.

John is mortified for a brief moment then turns happily to Barbara

John Still is, actually. (*As though introducing himself*) Mrs Smith! Hallo! Nice to meet you. How are you?

John shakes Barbara's hand profusely. Barbara is bemused. John smiles happily from Barbara to Vicki. Vicki is on the verge of tears

(*To Barbara*) And I believe you've already met my ... (*he realizes*) my ... my ... (*To Vicki*) And you've met my — my goodness it's warm today. Summer's come at last. Thought it never would. Same every year, isn't it? Rotten June and July, then "phew"!! (*He smiles brightly at Vicki*)

Vicki starts to cry

(*To Barbara*) Well, Miss — er — Smith has to rush off on her bike because someone has fallen off the roof. Boom!

Vicki (*in tears*) It's terrible. It's Uncle Stanley.

Vicki breaks down in tears, grabs her helmet and rushes out with her bicycle. She doesn't realize that she's left her shoulder bag behind in the armchair DRC

Barbara (*totally bemused*) What on earth's happened?

John (*innocently*) What?

Barbara You said someone had fallen off a roof.

John Oh, yes, that. Miss Smith's Uncle Stanley — that's Mr Gardner, their lodger, has fallen off the roof of their house in Wimbledon ... Kerboom! Completely ruined the flower bed. Miss Smith's father, Mr Smith, just popped over to tell her.

Barbara Mr Smith? Here?

John Yes! That's the other Mr Smith — from Wimbledon, nothing like me. Tall — skinny fellow — bit of a baldy. He couldn't stay. He had to get back to tidy up the flower bed.

Barbara What about Uncle Stanley?

John I'm sure he'll give a hand if he's up to it.

Barbara I mean, is he seriously injured?

John Mr Smith didn't go into details. Well, life must go on! I've got to pick up my old age pensioner from Tesco's.

Barbara Don't forget you're dining out tonight.

John Lovely. I'll ask him what he wants.

John hurries out through the Streatham front door

Barbara (*calling after*) John! I'd better ring Mrs Smith and tell her Vicki's on her way ...

John has already gone

Gavin appears in the ajar Wimbledon front door

Gavin Mr Smith?!

Gavin enters and closes the Wimbledon front door, as Barbara closes the Streatham front door

(*Calling upstairs*) Mr Smith!

Gavin hurries upstairs

Barbara moves down and picks up the print-out to check the number. She sits in the R corner of the settee

Stanley enters marching Gavin down the stairs

Stanley (*as he enters*) What are you doing back here, Gavin?!
Gavin Vicki wasn't in Poppy's Tea Rooms.
Stanley She will be!
Gavin No, I asked if anybody had seen a visually impaired girl with a white stick.
Stanley Gavin! Go back to Poppy's!

Barbara starts to dial

Gavin What's the point?
Stanley The coffee's brilliant!
Gavin I want to see Vicki.
Stanley You're obstinate as your bloody father, aren't you?
Gavin (*pleasantly surprised*) Do you know my dad?

Stanley hesitates

Stanley (*suddenly crying*) No!

The Wimbledon phone rings. Stanley looks anxiously to the kitchen then quickly picks up the phone

Barbara Hallo?
Stanley (*into the phone*) Wrong number! (*He bangs the phone down*)

During the following, Barbara double checks the number, re-dials and sits on the DR arm of settee

Gavin How did you know that was a wrong number?
Stanley I can tell by the ring. Off you go to Poppy's.
Gavin I told you. Vicki's not there.
Stanley She'll be there by now!
Gavin It was half an hour ago when you said she left ——
Stanley (*grabbing him*) Gavin!
Gavin (*pressing on*) —— and Poppy's Tea Rooms is only a five minutes walk.

Stanley (*shaking Gavin; yelling*) The girl can't see! It takes longer!
Gavin Well, even if it took her fifteen minutes ——
Stanley (*yelling*) I hate you, Gavin!! (*He furiously shakes Gavin*)

Mary enters from the kitchen carrying a loaf of bread on a bread board.
She stops, amazed on seeing Stanley shaking Gavin

I never want to see you again! Never! Ever!

Stanley realizes that Mary is standing in kitchen doorway. He stops shaking
Gavin, puts his arm around him and squeezes him affectionately

Mary looks outraged and storms back into the kitchen

Good-bye, Gavin!
Gavin No, I reckon Vicki will come back here.
Stanley Gavin, please!

Stanley drops to his knees and clasps Gavin around the waist

Mary enters from kitchen

Please! Please! Please!

Mary reacts to Stanley with his head apparently in Gavin's crotch. Finally,
Mary slams the door. Stanley slowly turns to Mary, puts his hands together
and prays to heaven

Mary storms into the dining-room

The phone rings. Stanley turns, looking apprehensive

Gavin Sounds like the same ring! (*He goes to lift the receiver*)

Stanley leaps to the phone and puts it to his ear

Barbara (*into the phone*) Mrs Smith, please!

Stanley indicates for Gavin to go. Gavin indicates that he's staying. During
the following, Stanley picks up the base of the phone, moves to the dining-
room door and locks it

(*Into the phone*) Hallo!
Stanley (*into the phone*) Hallo?

Barbara (*into the phone*; *with surprise*) Is that Mr Smith?
Stanley (*into the phone*) Er — yes.
Barbara (*into the phone*) You must have got home pretty quickly.
Stanley (*into the phone*; *with confusion*) Er — yes.
Barbara I was expecting to speak to your wife, actually.
Stanley Oh, yes.
Barbara Is she there?
Stanley Er — no.
Barbara (*into the phone*) I'm sorry I missed you when you were over here just now.
Stanley (*into the phone*; *confused*) Er — yes. (*To Gavin*) It's my bank manager. Wants to lend me some money. (*Into the phone*) Yes?

Stanley, to get away from Gavin, moves DLC

Barbara (*into the phone*) How were things when you got home?
Stanley (*into the phone*) Er — not good.
Barbara (*into the phone*) Oh, dear. Mr Gardner didn't die, did he?

Stanley considers this

Stanley (*into the phone*) Not yet, no.
Barbara (*into the phone*) Have they taken the poor man to hospital?
Stanley (*into the phone*) Any minute now!

Gavin, intrigued, has moved down to beside Stanley. Stanley sees him

  (*To Gavin*) I really don't require a loan of ten thousand, you know. (*He takes a step away from Gavin*; *into the phone*) But thank you for asking.
Barbara (*into the phone*) I suppose he shouldn't have been up on the roof in the first place.

Stanley is now even more confused

Stanley (*into the phone*) No-oo.
Barbara (*into the phone*) Just how far did Mr Gardner fall?
Stanley (*into the phone*) He didn't actually fall, he jumped.
Barbara That's terrible!
Stanley (*to Gavin*) Talking about a friend of mine.
Barbara (*into the phone*) What on earth drove him to that?
Stanley (*into the phone*) He couldn't settle his overdraft. (*To Gavin*) And they expect me to borrow money from them. (*Into the phone*) I must go now.

Barbara rises

Barbara (*into the phone*) Of course. You must be up to your eyes in it there.

Stanley (*into the phone*) Further than that. Bye, bye.

Barbara (*into the phone*) Oh, very quickly. Your Vicki should be with you any minute now.

Stanley (*into the phone; worried*) What?

Barbara (*into the phone*) She left on her bike a good ten minutes ago.

Stanley (*into the phone*) No!

Barbara (*into the phone*) What is it? What's happened?

Stanley (*calling out*) Can't you be more careful, Sharon! (*In a high-pitched voice*) Sorry, Mr Wilkinson, I don't know what's ——

Stanley stops as he realizes that Sharon is part of his Vodafone situation. Barbara and Gavin just look perplexed

(*Into the phone*) Thank you so much for calling and for your kind attention.

Stanley moves to above the L *end of the settee to replace the phone, as Barbara moves to above the* R *end of settee*

Barbara (*into the phone*) Oh, Mr Smith!

Stanley (*into the phone; with false patience*) Ye—es?

Stanley sits on the L *end of the settee, as Barbara sits on the* R *end of the settee*

Barbara (*into the phone*) I bet you got a good laugh when you discovered there was another John Smith here in Streatham.

During the following, Dad, angry, appears at the top of the stairs struggling with his stick and his suitcase

Gavin, but not Stanley, sees Dad and goes to assist by trying to relieve Dad of his suitcase. Dad doesn't want any assistance but Gavin persists. They struggle on the stairs with the suitcase being pulled to and fro

Stanley (*into the phone; falsely laughing*) Yes!

Barbara (*into the phone*) We must meet up one day.

Stanley (*into the phone; still laughing*) No!

Barbara (*into the phone*) No, I expect you're as busy as *my* John.

Stanley (*into the phone*) Yes!

Barbara (*into the phone*) My John never stops.

Stanley (*into the phone*) No!

Barbara (*into the phone; laughing*) I tell him he's got enough energy for two people.

Stanley (*into the phone; laughing*) Yes!

The struggle with Dad and Gavin concludes with Gavin pulling the suitcase from Dad's hand and Dad tumbling down the last of the stairs and falling flat on his face DLC. *Stanley turns*

(*Into the phone*) I must go now, the doctor's arrived. (*He bangs the phone down*)

Barbara replaces her receiver

Dad (*from the floor*) I don't want a doctor.

As Stanley and Gavin try to lift a truculent Dad, Barbara starts to walk towards the main bedroom but she stops when she sees Vicki's shoulder bag. During the following, Dad is helped to his feet

Barbara Oh, no. Silly girl. (*She picks the bag up, thinks for a moment, then goes to the phone, picks up the print-out, checks the number and dials*)
Dad I don't think much of this hotel, Stanley.
Stanley We're in Wimbledon!
Dad I thought we were going to Felixstowe!

Dad turns to Gavin who is standing there with Dad's suitcase

(*To Gavin*) Are you the porter in this place?
Gavin Er — no.
Dad Well, I want that taken to my room and a call at half past eight with a cup of tea.
Stanley Dad!
Gavin Oh. (*To Dad*) How do you do, sir. (*He holds out his hand*)
Dad You'll get a tip when I leave and not before. Cheeky blighter!
Gavin No, I was just going to shake your hand, Mr Smith.
Dad (*looking around*) Mr Smith?
Stanley Dad!

Stanley pulls Dad out of the way UL, *as the Wimbledon phone rings. Stanley looks at it in horror*

Dad Phone's ringing.

Stanley glares at Dad, lifts the receiver and listens

Barbara (*into the phone*) Hallo?

To Dad's surprise, Stanley replaces the receiver. Barbara, annoyed, starts to dial again

Stanley (*to Gavin*) I'm changing from Barclays to Lloyds. Right, Vicki's waiting for you.
Gavin I told you. She wasn't at Poppy's.
Stanley Ohhh! You didn't go to *Poppy's*, did you? I said Luigi's.
Gavin You said Poppy's.
Stanley No. Luigi's. Luigi's Bistro. Poppy's Tea Rooms, Luigi's Bistro. Easily mistaken. Do you know where Luigi's is?
Gavin No.
Stanley Well, it's the opposite direction to Poppy's. You take a right down Kenilworth Avenue ——

The Wimbledon phone rings. Stanley looks at it and hesitates

Dad Phone's ringing.

Stanley glares at Dad and then, to Dad's surprise Stanley picks up the phone and immediately replaces the receiver

Stanley (*to Gavin*) I'm going to report Barclays for harassment!

Stanley pushes Gavin to the front door, as Barbara, furiously, dials again. Dad, intrigued, moves to the phone, waiting for it to ring

(*To Gavin*) So, Luigi's. Vicki will be getting anxious. *Right* down Kenilworth ——

The Wimbledon phone rings. Dad immediately picks it up

Dad (*into the phone*) Stop pestering us, Mr Barclay!

Stanley hurries down to Dad's L

Barbara (*into the phone*) Is that Mr Smith's house?
Dad (*into the phone*) And what if it is?
Stanley Dad!

Stanley tries to grab the phone but Dad shrugs him off

Barbara (*into the phone*) Who am I talking to?
Dad (*into the phone*) How do I know? I can't see who you're talking to, can I?

Stanley Give me the phone!

Dad shrugs him off

Barbara (*into the phone*) May I leave a message for Mr Smith?
Dad (*into the phone*) Go ahead, Mr Barclay.
Stanley Dad!

Dad furiously shrugs him off

Barbara (*into the phone*) Say Vicki left her purse behind.
Dad (*into the phone*) Left Perce behind, right.
Barbara (*into the phone*) And I'm coming over to Wimbledon right now
with the purse. Your address is on the print-out.
Dad (*into the phone*) Got it, Mr Barclay. Bye, bye, Mr Barclay.

Dad puts the phone down

> *Barbara, bewildered, shakes her head and hurries out through the*
> *Streatham front door with the shoulder bag and the print-out*

(*To Stanley*) Mr Barclay says he's going to Wolverhampton with his
friend, Perce.

Stanley tries to work this out

Stanley (*confused*) What?
Dad He says —— (*He stops*) He's got a very high-pitched voice, your Mr
Barclay.
Stanley Never mind, Dad!
Dad You don't get this personal service at NatWest, you know.

Dad wanders, UR

Stanley Gavin, go to Luigi's! They do a fantastic cappuccino. The treat's on
me. Keep the change.

Stanley takes a five pound note from his pocket

Dad I can't see any deckchairs in this place.
Gavin (*to Stanley; referring to Dad*) That's your dad, yeah?
Stanley Yes!
Gavin You've got quite a family, haven't you?

Stanley Yes!

Stanley turns Gavin to go as Mary bangs on the dining-room door

Mary (*off*) Hey! *This* door's locked now!
Stanley (*to Gavin*) I've had to lock her in again. Goodbye, Gavin.
Mary (*off*) Hey! (*She bangs very loudly on the dining-room door*)
Dad It's a bit noisy this hotel, isn't it?

More loud banging from Mary

Mary (*off*) Hey!
Dad (*shouting across*) Who's making all that row?

Gavin moves to Dad

Gavin (*to Dad*) I'm afraid your daughter-in-law's having another turn.
Dad (*with delight*) Have I got a daughter-in-law?

Stanley pulls Gavin across him

Stanley Thank you, Gavin!
Dad Was I at the wedding, Stanley?
Stanley Yes! Good-bye, Gavin!
Gavin You don't think Vicki might have left Luigi's by now?
Stanley No, she's mad keen to see you. When I say "see" you ——
Gavin Well, if I miss her, I'll come straight back here.
Stanley No, please don't come straight back here, Gavin!

Stanley pushes Gavin to the front door

Gavin (*stopping*) Maybe I should *ring* your daughter first.
Dad (*to Stanley*) A daughter as well? Blimey, that was quick. You crafty little
    devil.
Stanley (*to Dad*) Go back upstairs!

Stanley pulls Dad across him to the stairs. Dad starts to go upstairs

Gavin Does Vicki have a mobile?
Stanley No, just a white stick and a guide dog. Go to Luigi's! (*He opens the
    front door to push Gavin out*)

   Mary is standing in the doorway, fuming. She storms in

Mary I had to climb out through the window!

Dad (*coming downstairs*) We're not on fire, are we?

Mary (*to Stanley; referring to Gavin*) I thought he'd gone!

Stanley He came back for some more. (*To Gavin*) Thanks for everything.

Stanley gives Gavin the five pound note. Mary reacts in amazement. Stanley realizes the implication and nearly dies. He pushes Gavin out

Gavin exits

(*Calling*) Remember, right, left, right! (*To Mary; army fashion*) Right, left, right, left!

Mary Stanley, that dining-room door is locked.

Stanley Why did you do that?

Mary I didn't do it!

Mary moves to the dining-room door to unlock it

Dad (*to Mary*) Excuse me, are you my daughter-in-law?

Mary (*trying to be polite*) No, I am not, Mr Gardner.

Dad I know you're not Mr Gardner, *I'm* Mr Gardner. (*To Stanley*) This hotel receptionist's a bit thick. (*To Mary*) And I don't see any sign saying "lavatory" in your hotel.

Mary (*to Dad; edgily*) I'm Mrs Smith. Nice to see you again.

Dad I've stayed here before, have I?

Stanley Go and have a rest, Dad!

Mary (*to Dad*) Would you like a cup of tea, Mr Gardner?

Dad Yes, please. A large whisky, no ice.

Mary Large whisky, no ice!

Mary unlocks the dining-room door and opens it

Vicki enters through the Wimbledon front door, still wearing her helmet, and pushing her bike

Vicki I got here as quick as I —— ! (*She sees Stanley; amazed*) Uncle Stan! You're upright.

Mary That's a matter of opinion!

Mary exits into the dining-room

Vicki (*to Stanley*) Dad said you were nearly dead.

Stanley Stick around!

Stanley crosses Vicki to DRC *followed by Vicki*

Vicki Aren't you going to see a doctor?
Stanley I'll wait till tomorrow. Things will be worse by then.

Stanley collapses in the armchair DRC. *Dad moves* DLC

Dad What's the matter, son? Your piles playing up again?
Stanley Go upstairs!
Vicki (*moving to Dad*) Hallo, Mr Gardner.
Dad You'll have to speak up, Nurse.
Vicki No, it's Vicki!
Dad Yes, rub some of that in. Do him good.
Stanley (*rising; to Dad*) You! Upstairs!

Stanley grabs Dad as Vicki looks in the mirror R *applying lipstick*

Dad (*cantankerously*) All right, all right! I can manage!
Stanley No, you can't!
Dad I'm not senile, you know, Rover!
Stanley Stanley!
Dad That was your mother's idea. I always wanted a dog.

Stanley starts to push a struggling Dad towards the stairs

Dad And I want my suitcase!
Stanley You don't need your suitcase.

Dad grabs his suitcase

Dad Course I do. I want my costume if I'm going for a swim.
Stanley You don't need your costume!

Dad stops

Dad It's not a topless beach. Is it?
Stanley We're not in Felixstowe!
Dad Where are we then?
Stanley Wimbledon!
Dad There's no beach in Wimbledon!
Stanley Get off!

Stanley pushes Dad off upstairs with his suitcase

   Dad exits

Vicki Right, I'm going!
Stanley Lovely. Nice long cycle ride round Wimbledon Common.
Vicki (*moving to the front door*) No. I'm going back to Gavin's house.

Stanley rushes down the stairs and takes a surprised Vicki DRC

Stanley What? No!
Vicki I bet he's back there by now. And I was getting on very well with his mum.

Stanley hesitates

Stanley (*aghast*) You met Gavin's mum?
Vicki Yeah! His dad should be home by now as well.

Vicki moves in front of Stanley. Stanley grabs her

Stanley No!
Vicki Don't *you* start! I'm going to meet Gavin.

Stanley pulls Vicki across

Stanley Vicki, please! You mustn't go back to Gavin's house. (*Madly thinking*) I mean you — er — you don't have to go there. Gavin's waiting for you!
Vicki What?
Stanley Gavin's waiting for you. In a café. Round the corner. He asked me to tell you.
Vicki Well, why didn't you?
Stanley (*shouting*) I fell off the roof, didn't I?!
Vicki Well, which café?
Stanley Do you know Poppy's Tea Rooms?
Vicki In the High Street, yeah.
Stanley Yes. Left down Kenilworth. Right at the High Street. Poppy's is on the left.
Vicki I know it. Yes!
Stanley Whatever you do, don't go *right, left, right*.
Vicki No!
Stanley That's where Luigi's is. Dreadful place, Luigi's. Worst cappuccino in Wimbledon.
Vicki OK!

Vicki crosses in front of Stanley to below the settee

John bursts in through the front door. Once more he is totally out of breath. He moves to DLC

John Visitors? Any visitors?

Stanley crosses Vicki

Stanley (*pointedly*) *Visitors* all dealt with!
John Thank heavens!

John collapses in the armchair DLC

Stanley Yes. So off you toddle, Vicki.

Stanley takes Vicki's hand and starts to pull her ULC

John Where's she going?
Vicki (*stopping*) I'm meeting Gavin.

John jumps up and grabs Vicki

John What?!

Stanley moves down to L *of the armchair and sits John down*

Stanley It's all right!
Vicki Now don't come "the heavy father" again. I'm going to meet Gavin!
John (*rising*) You can't!

Stanley sits John down again

Stanley John, it's for the best.
John You keep out of this!
Stanley No, I mean it'll give all of us some *time*. Gavin's waiting for her at *Poppy's Tea Rooms*.
John (*rising*) She's not going!
Vicki Yes, I am!
John No, you're not!

Stanley sits John forcefully and then kneels at John's feet

Stanley (*pleading*) Yes, she is! We need *time*! That's why she's going to see Gavin at *Poppy's* — not *Luigi's*, that's a filthy place!

John (*rising*) She's not meeting him anywhere! She can't! She mustn't!
Vicki Don't start that again!

During the ensuing tirade, an increasingly crazed Stanley, still on his knees, crawls up John's legs, grabs him by the lapels, pulls him across and bangs John's head against the kitchen door. At the same time a bewildered Vicki backs up towards the front door

Stanley (*suddenly furious*) No, don't start that again! She's meeting Gavin at Poppy's! It's a good idea. It's the best idea I've had all day. It's bloody brilliant! Poppy's Tea Rooms! Left, right, left. Not right, left, right. Poppy's not Luigi's! Luigi's Bistro does the foulest cappuccino in Wimbledon! (*To Vicki; yelling*) Now, piss off to Poppy's!

Stanley pushes a surprised Vicki out with her bicycle

Vicki exits

Stanley, emotionally drained, collapses in the armchair DR, *while John staggers round, dazed, holding his head, ending up* DLC

John (*finally; aghast*) What have you done?
Stanley What I've been doing all afternoon! Giving myself a heart attack.
John You've sent her round to Poppy's Tea Rooms!
Stanley Because Gavin's waiting for her at Luigi's!
John (*realizing*) Stanley, I love you! (*He hugs Stanley*)

Mary comes in from the dining-room with Dad's whisky. She sees Stanley and John cuddling

They don't see her. Mary slams the dining-room door furiously. John and Stanley slowly turn to Mary. Stanley removes himself from John's arms

Stanley (*to Mary*) I was giving John ——

Mary backs Stanley to DRC

Mary (*interrupting*) I'd rather not know what you were giving John, thank you very much. And I suggest you stick to young men, if you don't mind.
Stanley No, Mary, love, you see ——
Mary Don't you "love" me! (*Tersely*) Where's your father?
Stanley He's upstairs.

Mary Give him that. (*She thrusts the whisky at Stanley*) He'll need it when
I tell him what a degenerate son he's got. (*To John*) Are you staying or
going?

John Er — going. Yes. Definitely. Pick up this old age pensioner from
Tesco's.

John opens the kitchen door

Mary Haven't you done that job yet?

John (*at a loss*) We keep missing each other.

John pushes Mary into the kitchen

  Mary exits

Stanley This started off as such a lovely day.

*Stanley sits on the R arm of the settee, drinks the whisky and puts the glass on
the table R of the settee*

John Don't worry.

John locks the kitchen door

  I'll put Mary straight later on.

Stanley I don't think I'll ever be straight again.

John crosses DRC to Stanley

John Right. Gavin's waiting for Vicki in Luigi's, yeah?

Stanley Hopefully, yes!

John lifts Stanley

John OK. You go down to Luigi's and tell Gavin ——

Stanley I'm going to Felixstowe with Dad!

John Don't be difficult, Stanley. Tell Gavin he's to get back to Streatham
right away. There's been a robbery in Lewin Road, I've been arrested for
it, the police are questioning me and his mother wants him back there right
away.

Stanley (*interrupting*) Wait a minute, wait a minute!

John Say anything but get Gavin to Streatham!

Stanley It was difficult enough getting him to Luigi's!

John Look, while you're dealing with Gavin, I'll go round to Poppy's and tell Vicki we've had a gas explosion here, the kitchen's ended up in the next door neighbour's garden and we've got to go and stay with friends in the Shetland Islands.

Stanley backs DR

Stanley (*interrupting*) Hold it, hold it, hold it! (*Seriously*) You can't keep this up forever. Face it. Those kids intend to meet. Sooner or later your wives will meet. The game is over.

John moves to Stanley

John Don't you believe it. The game's not over till the final whistle blows. Remember what Shakespeare said ——!

Dad enters from upstairs

Dad (*as he enters*) Your ballcock's not working, Stanley! (*He moves* DLC)

They slowly look to Dad

John Or words to that effect.

Dad has arrived DLC. *Stanley crosses to Dad*

Stanley What's the problem, Dad?!
Dad I spent a penny and I can't stop the flow. (*He laughs*) The flow of the lavatory, I mean, not the flow of ——
Stanley (*interrupting*) I know what you mean!
John You only have to jiggle the handle up and down.

Dad crosses to John

Dad (*to John*) Are you the manager of this hotel?
John I'm Mr Smith!
Dad Mr Smith? My son lodges with a Mr Smith. Lovely fellow — I know him well.

Stanley pulls Dad across him to DLC

Stanley Go back upstairs!
Dad No, I think I'll go for a stroll along the promenade. (*He starts to wander towards the front door*)

Stanley Dad!
John (*moving to Stanley*) Never mind your dad. You go and grab Gavin from
   Luigi's. I'll sort out Vicki in Poppy's.

Dad opens the front door

   Gavin enters

Gavin (*as he enters*) Mr Smith! Mr Smith!
John Ahhh!

*John about turns and dives face down on to the floor in front of the settee
before Gavin can see him. Gavin arrives* DL. *Stanley quickly moves very close
to Gavin to mask him from John*

Stanley Hi. Gav!
Gavin It's shut.
Stanley What's shut, Gavin?
Gavin Luigi's.
Stanley Probably opens at six.
Gavin No, there's a notice on the door. They're closed for redecorating. I bet
   you it was Poppy's Tea Rooms after all.

Gavin moves US *and Stanley quickly moves with him, still nose to nose. Dad
now notices the prostrate John*

Stanley (*grabbing him*) No! It wasn't Poppy's. Definitely.
Gavin I'll get on the motorbike and be there in two minutes.
Stanley That's a terrible idea, Gavin.
Gavin Yeah, might miss her. Better wait here.

Gavin moves DS *a pace and Stanley moves with him*

Stanley That's even worse!!

Dad taps Stanley on the shoulder. Stanley turns to him

Dad (*pointing to John*) I think the manager has collapsed.
Stanley Dad!

Stanley closes his eyes in anguish. Gavin steps forward to look

Gavin (*to Stanley*) Hey, isn't that your brother-in-law, Stanley?

Stanley Yes!

Dad His brother-in-law, "Stanley"?

Stanley (*to Gavin*) Yes. He was sleepwalking again — and he fell off the roof — boom.

Gavin Blimey!

Gavin goes to look but Stanley drags him back

Stanley Yes, he staggered in here then collapsed.

Gavin Let's pick him up and put him on the settee.

Gavin moves towards John again, but Stanley drags him back

Stanley No! Sadly — (*he quickly covers John's head and shoulders with the throw from the back of the settee*) — he's dead.

Gavin Dead?

Stanley Yes.

Gavin Blimey.

Gavin crosses Stanley to look but Stanley pushes him DR. During the following, Dad moves to ULC watching

Stanley We tried to revive him, but unfortunately, only moments ago, he succumbed. Gavin, go in there — (*he points to the second bedroom*) — and get a sheet off the bed, will you?

Gavin A sheet?

Stanley Yes. He really should be completely covered.

Gavin Don't you need a doctor?

Stanley I certainly do.

Gavin No, for him. He should be certified, shouldn't he?

Stanley Definitely! It's all in hand. Get the sheet, Gavin. (*He opens the second bedroom door*)

Gavin Why don't I try giving him the kiss of life first?

Gavin moves to the body

Stanley (*quickly stopping Gavin*) No! He's definitely dead.

Gavin He might not be. I did a survival course at school.

Stanley Yes, you bloody would, Gavin!

Gavin It's worth a try.

Gavin moves to the body again

Stanley (*quickly stopping Gavin*) No!

Gavin It must be. (*He moves to the body again*)

Stanley (*quickly stopping Gavin*) No! (*He pushes Gavin* DR) He's my
brother-in-law. (*He marches around the prone John and stands astride
him*) If anyone's going to give him the kiss of life, it'll be me! (*Masking
John's face from Gavin with the throw, he turns John over. He hesitates,
gulps, takes a big breath, closes his eyes and descends on John covering
their heads with the throw. He proceeds to give John a prolonged and
exaggerated kiss of life*)

Dad Blimey, if he's not dead, that'll kill him off. (*He sits on the* R *arm of the
armchair* DLC)

Stanley, out of breath, comes up for air — still masking John's face

Gavin You have to do longer than that.

*Stanley glares at Gavin, then pounces on John again giving him another
exaggerated kiss of life*

Dad (*to Stanley*) I say, I bet you wish it was Joan Collins.

Stanley slowly comes up for air glaring at Dad then turns to Gavin

Stanley (*sadly*) It's no good, Gavin, he's dead.

Gavin moves towards Stanley

Gavin The book says you should give at least three minutes.

Stanley (*shouting*) He's bloody dead, Gavin! Now, please! Please show a
little respect for the deceased!

Stanley rolls John up in the rug. Gavin is aghast

Gavin You can't just roll him up in a carpet. (*He starts to move to John*)

Stanley grabs Gavin and marches him to the second bedroom

Stanley You're right. You can't just roll him up in a carpet. Go and get a
sheet!!

Gavin Yeah, OK! Oh. Does Auntie Rosie know yet?

Stanley She doesn't care, Gavin, she's potty! Get the sheet!

Gavin hurriedly exits into the second bedroom

John, furiously, rolls himself out of the carpet. Dad is amazed and rises staring at John who stands up with the throw dangling from his mouth

John That was a bit close, Stanley!
Stanley (*wiping his mouth*) Too bloody close, thank you.
John Lock Gavin in Vicki's bedroom.
Stanley God! (*He locks the second bedroom door*)
Dad (*gaping at John*) It's a miracle, not a scratch!

Dad sits in armchair DLC. The doorbell rings. John and Stanley react. Stanley hurries to John

Stanley Might be Vicki!
John Vicki?
Stanley Back from Poppy's — no Gavin there.
John Right, let's think!
Stanley *Now* he says, "think".

John's ensuing speech is delivered with speedy military precision. During the latter part of the speech, Stanley starts to go crossed-eyed and weakly backs away slowly towards the armchair DR. He feels for the armchair and sits, expressionless, staring at John

John OK! You go upstairs and look out of your bedroom windows. If it's Vicki tell her I've been taken to St Thomas's hospital with concussion — brought about when you banged my head on the kitchen door. She's to get over to the hospital right away. You go with her. While you're dealing with Vicki, I'll go in there to Gavin, put on the "heavy father" act and say I've come over to Wimbledon to take him home to Streatham. As soon as you've dumped Vicki at the hospital get back here and tell Mary that I've had to go and pick up my old age pensioner from Tesco's. I'll take Barbara out to that new vegetarian restaurant in Streatham — better take Gavin with us — yes. Then as soon as we've sat down to dinner, I'll say I've suddenly remembered my old age pensioner at Tesco's and get back here for a quick lamb stew with Mary. OO! As soon as you've dumped Vicki at the hospital — but before you come back here to tell Mary I've gone to pick up my old age pensioner from Tesco's — ring up the AA. You ring the AA and tell them to get over here right away and fix the puncture on my taxi. By the time they've done that I'll be back here with Mary and the lamb stew and you and your dad can have your car and push off to Felixstowe. (*To Stanley*) You got that?

Stanley shakes his head. Dad rises

Dad I got it, it's brilliant!

Stanley rises

Stanley It's terrible!

The doorbell rings again. John and Stanley react. John pulls Stanley across him and URC

John Upstairs. If it's Vicki, St Thomas's hospital. I'll go in there to Gavin and, as soon as you've dealt with Vicki, I'll get him back to Streatham.

The doorbell rings again. Dad moves ULC

Dad (*to Stanley*) I'm getting a bit worried, you know.
Stanley (*confused*) What?
Dad I keep hearing this ringing sound in my ears

The kitchen door is banged

Mary (*off*) Have you locked me in *again*, Stanley?!
Stanley Of course, it's bound to be me.
John Upstairs!

John pushes Stanley upstairs. There is more banging on the kitchen door

Mary (*off*) Hey!
Dad (*to John*) I'm going to make an official complaint about the noise in your hotel.
John (*to Stanley*) Upstairs. See if it's Vicki.

The kitchen door is banged

Mary (*off*) Open this door!
Dad (*calling*) Shut up!

The second bedroom door is banged

Gavin (*off*) Hey, this door seems to be locked!
Dad And you can shut up as well.
John (*to Stanley*) I'll deal with Gavin and Mary.

The doorbell rings

    And if that's Vicki ——
Stanley I know! You're in St Thomas's hospital expecting a baby!

Stanley exits upstairs

Mary (*off*) If you don't open this door, Stanley, I'm going to kick it in!

The kitchen door is kicked. John decides on the kitchen door. The doorbell rings

Dad (*banging his ear*) Blast, blast it, blast it!

Dad moves to the stairs. John unlocks the kitchen door

    Mary storms in with a carving knife

Mary Stanley, if you lock me ——! (*She stops*) John! Did you *lock* that door?
John No, Stanley did.
Mary Right! He's had it now!

Mary runs past John to the stairs but comes face to face with Dad. Dad reacts to the pointed knife and puts his hands in the air

Dad (*cowering from her*) Ahhh! Guest! Guest!
John Mary! Never mind Stanley. (*He takes the carving knife from Mary and puts it on the table behind the settee*) I've got this splitting headache. Could you find the aspirins for me?
Mary Can't you get your own aspirins?
John No. I'm in the middle of fixing the upstairs lavatory. Water everywhere.
Dad (*still with his hands in the air*) That's the ballcock, not me.
John Mary, please! Aspirins. In our bedside cabinet.
Mary (*to John*) No. I left them in Vicki's room. (*She moves towards the second bedroom*)

John grabs Mary

John No!
Mary Yes, I did. I'll get them.
John No! I mean, "no" I don't want any aspirins.
Mary You said you had a splitting headache.
John I have but the stomach pain is worse. Terrible. OO! Tummy stuff —
bedside cabinet.

John starts to move Mary to the main bedroom, but Mary moves URC

Mary Hang on. Didn't I hear the front doorbell just now?

John rushes up to Mary

John Yes. Jehovah's Witness.
Mary What?
John Jehovah's Witness. I got rid of them.

The doorbell rings

They're so bloody persistent, aren't they? (*He holds his stomach*) OO!
Quick. Tummy stuff.

John starts to move Mary DR, *but there are bangs from the second bedroom.*
Mary stops

Gavin (*off*) Will someone unlock this door!
Mary (*with surprise*) That's Stanley's young bloke.
John Yes.
Mary (*increasingly surprised*) What's he doing in that bedroom?
John Well, he wanted to leave but Stanley wouldn't let him.
Mary (*with outrage*) So Stanley locked him in Vicki's bedroom?
John He's besotted with the boy.
Dad And he's got Mr Barclay and Perce coming any minute now.
John Thank you! (*He pushes Mary down to the main bedroom*)

   Stanley, excited, rushes down the stairs

Stanley It's all right, John —— ! (*He sees Mary; sweetly*) Hallo, Mary.
Mary I'll deal with you later, Stanley Gardner!

   Mary exits into the main bedroom

Stanley Now what have you told her?

John locks the main bedroom door. He and Stanley meet below the settee, C

John Never mind! Is that Vicki at the front door?
Stanley No, you're all right. It's just some lady.
John What lady?
Stanley I don't know what lady!

Dad I do. It's Jehovah's waitress.

Stanley and John look at Dad and he smiles

Got to have your wits about you, Stanley.

The doorbell rings

John (*to Stanley*) Did you ask her what she wants?
Stanley No. She'll go away if we don't answer it. I think she came in a little green car.
John (*worried*) Green car?
Stanley Yes. Parked outside.
John (*agog*) Is she tall, reddish hair and big boobs?
Stanley Yeah. Lovely, eh? (*He squeezes imaginary boobs*)
John (*with horror*) It's Barbara!
Stanley You lucky sod! (*He squeezes again then realizes*) Barbara?!
John Yes!
Stanley You mean "wife" Barbara?!
John Yes! What the hell's she doing in Wimbledon?!
Dad Do you think Barbara would let me —— (*He squeezes imaginary boobs*)
Stanley Go upstairs!

The doorbell rings. Dad bangs his ears

Dad (*to Stanley*) What's it called, this ringing in the ears?
Stanley Tinnitus!
John Never mind "Tinnitus"! You've got to deal with Barbara.
Stanley Why can't *you* deal with Barbara?
John Because I'm dealing with Gavin and Mary!

The doorbell rings urgently

Dad Blast this rin tin tin.

As Dad starts to walk upstairs, there is banging from Gavin

Gavin (*off*) Anybody there? I've got the sheet!
John (*to Stanley*) I'll do Gavin. You do Barbara. Go upstairs and strip off.
Stanley Strip off?!
John Then open your bedroom window and call down to Barbara ——
Stanley Wait a minute —— !

John Tell her you're Mr Smith, you're having a bath, there's nobody else in the house and get rid of her!
Stanley John!
John Go on, strip off and sort out Barbara.
Stanley (*firmly*) No. I won't sort out Barbara.
Dad I'll sort out Barbara!

Dad happily squeezes imaginary boobs and exits quickly upstairs

Stanley Dad!

Stanley exits upstairs

There are bangs from Gavin in the second bedroom

Gavin (*off*) Hey!

John takes a breath and moves towards the second bedroom. There are bangs from the main bedroom. John stops

Mary (*off*) Hey, *this* bloody door's locked now!
John (*calling*) Yes, that was Stanley.
Mary (*off*) Silly sod!
John (*calling*) I don't know what's come over him today.
Mary (*off*) I've got the stuff for your stomach!
John (*calling*) I'll go and ask Stanley what he's done with the key.
Mary (*off*) I'll kill him!
Gavin (*off*) Hey!

Gavin bangs on his door. John adopts a "heavy father" attitude and unlocks the door

Gavin enters carrying a sheet

Gavin I hope this is big enough —— (*He stops*) Dad!
John Come on, my lad! Home!
Gavin What the hell are *you* doing here?

John moves Gavin towards the front door

John Getting you out of this house! (*He quickly stops*) And we'll go the back way through the kitchen. (*He takes Gavin below the settee*)
Gavin Don't be daft! Hey! Where's Mr Gardner gone? (*He points to the floor*)

John Upstairs. Taking a bath.

John turns Gavin but Gavin turns back

Gavin I thought he was dead.

John considers this

John The other Mr Smith is cleaning Mr Gardner up before the undertaker calls. Come on, you're not staying in this house a moment longer.
Gavin Why not for God's sake?
John I've done my checks, son. That email from Vicki was really sent by a perverted old Internet weirdo ——
Gavin A perverted old ——
John —— Internet weirdo who passes himself off as a fifteen-year-old schoolgirl.

Gavin marches purposefully past John to DR

Gavin No. This address was on that print-out.

John hurries to Gavin

John That's right. This old pervert lives here.
Gavin What?
John Yes!
Gavin Where is he then?

Dad enters from upstairs

Dad You're not kidding they're beauties!!

Dad squeezes imaginary boobs. John's face breaks into a smile and he indicates to Gavin that Dad is the "old pervert". John then smiles at Dad who smiles back and repeats the imaginary squeezing. John looks back to Gavin

Gavin (*amazed*) You mean Mr Smith's old dad sent me the emails signed "Vicki"?

John grabs the sheet from Gavin

John Yeah. You don't want to stay here another second.

John turns Gavin, but Gavin is rooted to the spot

Gavin So Vicki doesn't know anything about me then?

John pulls Gavin across and pushes him to the kitchen. During the following, Dad picks up the newspaper from the chest of drawers LC, moves to the settee DRC, and sits on the R end of the settee

John Not a thing. Through the kitchen. On your bike and get the hell out of here.
Gavin Wait a minute, though. Mr Smith said Vicki was waiting for me in a café.
John Ah, yes. Mr Smith explained that to me. Little white lie. He wanted to get you away from the house — to keep you out of the clutches of his dad. (*He indicates Dad*)

Dad happily waves at them and repeats the "squeezing"

Quick, go while the going's good. I'll see you at home, son.

John opens the kitchen door

Gavin Aren't *you* coming?
John No. I told Mr Smith I'd help him with Mr Gardner's funeral arrangements.

Gavin looks crestfallen. John pushes him out through the kitchen door, leaving the door ajar

Gavin exits

Stanley hurries down the stairs dressed in a towel. He meets John DLC

Stanley (*in a panic*) John, John, I can't get Barbara to go!
John What?!
Stanley She's brought Vicki's purse.
Dad No, I think you'll find Perce is with Mr Barclay.
John (*to Stanley*) Tell her to leave it on the front step and go!
Stanley She wants to come in and say "hallo" to the other Mrs Smith.
John So you told her she couldn't!
Stanley No. I said I'd go and see if Mary was available.
John What?!
Stanley I was getting all nervous!

John (*furiously*) Why didn't you just say that Mary was on holiday in North Africa and wasn't expected back until next year?
Stanley (*almost weeping*) Because that never entered my head!

Banging is heard on the main bedroom door

Mary (*off*) Hey! John, have you got that key from Stanley?

John hurries towards main bedroom

John (*calling*) Stanley's run off with it!
Stanley That's lovely!

Dad rises

Dad (*to Stanley; referring to the towel*) If you're going for a swim, son, I'll come with you. (*He moves to John*) What time's high tide here?
John Any minute now! (*He crosses to Stanley*) Go back upstairs and call down to Barbara that Mary has suddenly been taken very ill ——
Stanley (*protesting*) John —— !
John Very, very ill.
Dad I reckon it's the air in Felixstowe, you know.

John and Stanley look at Dad

Well, one ill, one dead and me with my tetanus.
Stanley Tinnitus!
Mary (*off*) Hey!

There are bangs from Mary as Dad wanders URC

John (*to Stanley*) I'll deal with Mary! Tell Barbara anything but get rid of her!

John pushes Stanley ULC *and during the following returns* C *below the settee*

Stanley (*angrily*) Why don't I just say that everybody's gone to Stanley Gardner's funeral!

Stanley exits upstairs as Barbara appears in the half-open kitchen doorway. She is carrying Vicki's shoulder bag

Barbara (*as she enters; calling*) Mrs Smith … ?! Mrs Smith … ?!

John (*yelling*) Ahhh! (*As he yells, he neatly throws the sheet over his head, completely enveloping himself*)

Barbara sees John in the sheet

Stanley hurries in from upstairs to DLC

Stanley (*as he enters, with elation*) John, it's all right, she's gone! (*He sees Barbara*) Oooo! (*He turns and sees John in the sheet*) Oooo!
Barbara I didn't mean to drag you out of your bath again.

Stanley tries to laugh and shrugs helplessly. Dad moves down to John's R *to look at the figure in the sheet*

I just thought I'd try the back door in case your wife was in the kitchen.

Dad is now more interested in Barbara. He gives her a naughty wink and squeezes imaginary boobs

Stanley And you've already met my father up in the window.
Barbara (*calling to Dad*) Hallo again.
Stanley And—er—you're probably wondering who—er ... (*He indicates John*) Yes. He fell off the roof.
Barbara (*referring to John*) Oh, he's your lodger.
Stanley Yes.
Barbara Terrible thing to happen.
Stanley Yes. And you're probably wondering why Mr Gardner's wearing a — er ...

There is a brief pause as Barbara waits for Stanley to explain the sheet

Yes! That is a thermal sheet. To keep Mr Gardner warm. After he fell off the roof his body temperature dropped — so we were advised to wrap Mr Gardner in a thermal sheet. There we are. Just finish off. Make sure it's air tight. (*He wraps the sheet tight around John. He then takes the bottom of the sheet and sharply pulls it up between John's legs*)
John (*painfully*) Ahh!
Stanley You all right, Mr Gardner? (*He pulls again*)
John Ahh!
Stanley I'm glad one of us is, Mr Gardner! (*He pulls again*)
John Ahh!

Dad crosses John to Stanley

Dad (*to Stanley*) Hang on a minute … Why do you keep calling Mr Smith,
Mr ——?

*Before he can finish, John neatly kicks Dad's stick from under him. The stick
goes flying and Dad falls to the floor but immediately gets up and starts to
shadow box an invisible assailant. He then collects his stick from* UR. *N.B. If
the actor paying Dad is unable to fall to the floor he can stumble around and
then sit in the* DRC *armchair*

Stanley (*to Barbara*) Bye, bye, Mrs Smith. It's been a great pleasure.
Barbara Well, actually, I'd quite like to say hallo to a fellow "Mrs John
Leonard Smith". Is she around?
Stanley No! My poor Mary is very, very, very ill. She's in bed, fast asleep
and you can't see her.
Barbara I'm sorry to hear that.
Stanley Yes.

*Stanley turns to Barbara to push her out. There are loud bangs from Mary
in the bedroom. Barbara turns back. The "sheeted" John, Stanley and Dad
look to the door*

Mary (*off*) Have you got that bloody key yet?

John and Stanley look at Barbara

Stanley (*to Barbara*) That's not Mary! That's Rosie. Rosie Gardner.
Married to Stanley Gardner. (*He points to John*) Rosie went potty about the
same time as Mary. Did I tell you that Mary was potty as well as being very,
very ill?
Barbara (*bemused*) No!

*There is banging from Mary. The "sheeted" John, Stanley and Dad look to
the door*

Mary (*off*) I'm going to kill you, Stanley Gardner.

John and Stanley look to Barbara

Stanley (*to Barbara*) Rosie has developed this pathological hatred of her
husband. As you can see we're a very dysfunctional family. Thanks for
calling and for your own safety don't come back.

Stanley crosses Barbara and opens the kitchen door

Barbara (*bemused*) I'll say goodbye then.
Stanley And you said it very nicely.

Stanley pushes Barbara out into the kitchen not realizing that she is still clutching Vicki's shoulder bag. He slams the door and leans against it

Barbara exits

Oh, my God!

John extricates himself from the sheet and throws the sheet into the armchair

John You're learning fast, Stanley.
Stanley I think I hate you as much as I hate Gavin.

Barbara returns holding out the shoulder bag

Barbara (*as she enters*) I say! You forgot to take Vicki's —— (*She stops*)

Immediately, John about turns and dives over the DRC armchair, from the front. His knees are on the seat and his bottom is sticking up in the air with his head and shoulders hanging over the back of the armchair. Stanley tries to smile

Stanley The five minutes on the thermal was up. Mustn't overdo the thermal. He's now doing his ten minutes yoga. Very therapeutic for those who've fallen off the roof. Brings the blood pressure right down — and the legs up. (*He pulls John's legs up*) Legs apart! (*He pulls them apart*)
John Ahh!
Stanley Nothing like it! Together — apart! Together — apart! Together — apart!
John Ahhh! Ahhh! Ahhh!
Stanley Wonderful. (*To Barbara*) Brings tears to your eyes, doesn't it?
Dad That reminds me. Is the lavatory working now?
Stanley Yes. Just jiggle it up and down!
Dad I always do when, when I've finished. Little shake.
Stanley The handle! (*To Barbara*) Thank you so much for bringing Vicki's purse back.

Stanley takes the shoulder bag from Barbara

Barbara (*to Stanley*) Don't the local council provide any nursing assistance for this household?
Stanley We don't need any assistance. (*He turns Barbara to go*)

Barbara (*turning back*) But with a disturbed wife, a deranged sister, an injured brother-in-law and an incapacitated father ——
Stanley That's my lot in life. I accept it!

Stanley turns Barbara but she resists

Barbara I think I could help, you know. I do stress counselling in my spare time.
Stanley Your son takes after you, doesn't he?!
Barbara (*accepting the "compliment"*) Thank you.

The main bedroom door is banged

Mary (*off*) If somebody doesn't open this door I'm going to kick it in.

The door is kicked

Dad I think Rosie's locked herself in the lavatory.
Stanley Dad!
Dad (*to the door*) Are you going to be long, Rosie? (*He bangs on the bedroom door*) There's a queue here!
Barbara (*to Stanley*) Why don't I take your father upstairs?

Barbara moves to the stairs as the bedroom door is kicked several times

Stanley Yes! I think that might be the best idea. While I deal with Rosie. Dad! Mrs Smith is taking you upstairs.
Dad OO, lovely! (*He mimes "squeezing" boobs and pushes Barbara upstairs*)

Dad and Barbara exit

John (*standing up*) What have you done?
Stanley I've been doing my best under very trying circumstances!
John We'll never get rid of Barbara now.
Stanley I wouldn't worry. Two minutes with Dad upstairs and she'll be out of here like a shot.

The main bedroom door is suddenly splintered open with a crash

Mary stumbles in with a medicine bottle

John Mary!

Mary Right! Where's Stanley!
Stanley Now, Mary … !
John Mary! Darling! Have you got my medicine?
Mary (*advancing on Stanley*) I'm going to give Stanley *his* medicine first!

Stanley backs

Stanley Mary!

John tries to restrain Mary

John Mary! Stanley's not himself today.
Stanley I should be so lucky. (*He realizes he's holding Vicki's shoulder bag and guiltily drops it onto the settee*)
Mary (*to John*) There's your tummy stuff. (*She thrusts the bottle at Stanley*)
John Thank you. Where's the aspirins?
Mary You said you didn't want aspirins.
John I must have aspirins! The pain! The pain!
Mary All right. They're in Vicki's room.
John Get them! (*He pushes Mary towards the second bedroom*)
Stanley No!!!!

John and Mary stop and look at him. Stanley realizes that Gavin is no longer in the second bedroom

(*Foolishly*) I'd forgotten. He's gone.

Mary opens the second bedroom door

Mary I can't believe what's happened in this house today.
Stanley Join the club.

Mary gives Stanley a withering look and exits into the second bedroom

John quickly locks the door

John Right, Stanley ——

John moves to Stanley. Barbara screams from upstairs

Barbara!
Barbara (*off*) Mr Smith!

John quickly steps into the cupboard under the stairs

Barbara appears at the top of the stairs clutching her bosom. She hurries down into the room

Barbara (*to Stanley*) Some of your father's faculties are still functioning.

Dad enters happily at the top of the stairs. He is clutching a rolled up towel in which are his swimming trunks

Dad I think this sea air's doing me good, you know!
Stanley Please, go and lie down!
Dad No. I'm going for a swim, and as there are ladies present, I shall change in the beach hut. (*He opens the cupboard door*)

John is standing there in a raincoat and hat with a scarf completely wrapped around his face and wearing sunglasses. He looks like the Invisible Man. He stands there for a moment then walks stiffly from the cupboard and out through the kitchen door

Barbara, open-mouthed, walks DRC staring after John. Stanley takes a deep breath and closes the kitchen door

Stanley I've told you about my mad Mary, potty Auntie Rosie and suicidal Uncle Stanley … ?

Barbara nods

That was crazy Cousin Cuthbert. (*He collapses into the armchair DLC*)

The kitchen door opens

John appears minus raincoat, scarf, sunglasses and hat. He leaves the kitchen door open and hurries to Barbara

John Right, let's go!
Barbara (*with surprise*) Johnny!
John Come on!

John pulls Barbara to below the settee C, but she stops

Barbara What on earth are you doing here?
John Getting you out of this place. I'll tell you all about it when I get you home.

John pulls Barbara towards the kitchen but she pulls back. John ends up on Stanley's L and Barbara on Stanley's R

Barbara Wait a minute. (*He points to Stanley*) Mr Smith has a lot to contend with here. This is a deprived home.
John None of our business!
Barbara It *should* be our business. (*To Stanley*) He doesn't know about your wife's mental problems, does he, Mr Smith?
Stanley (*shaking his head dumbly*) No.

There is banging from the second bedroom. They all look

During the following, Dad has puts his towel and costume on the table ULC and comes down to John's L

Mary (*off*) You've bloody locked me in *again*!
Barbara (*to Stanley*) Is that Mary or Rosie?
Stanley Take your pick.
Barbara (*to Stanley*) Shall I tell my husband about mad Mary, potty Auntie Rosie, suicidal Uncle Stanley and crazy Cousin Cuthbert?
Stanley Please don't.

Stanley shakes his head dumbly

John Mr Smith can deal with it, can't you, Mr Smith?

Stanley shakes his head. John quickly taps him and Stanley quickly nods his head

See, Mr Smith can deal with it!
Dad (*to John*) Why do you keep calling my son, Mr —— ?

Before Dad can finish, John kicks Dad's stick from under him and the stick goes flying R. Dad falls to the ground and then stands up boxing. John about-turns Dad and pushes him out into the kitchen

Dad exits

There is the extended sound of the crashing of crockery and saucepans

John Right, we're out of here.
Barbara (*to Stanley*) Will your father be all right?
Stanley Yes, crazy Cousin Cuthbert will look after him.

Stanley rises and crosses R *for Dad's stick. He leans the stick against the armchair* DRC

John (*to Barbara*) Right, we're out of here! (*He opens the kitchen door*)

Gavin walks straight in, very assertively

John is aghast. Stanley sits in the armchair DRC *and buries his head in his hands*

Gavin Poor old Mr Smith seems to be ——
John What are *you* doing here?
Gavin (*determined*) I'm sorry, Dad!
John Gavin!
Gavin I've been thinking about what … (*He crosses to Barbara*) Mum! What are you doing here?

John moves to Gavin

John I told you to go home, Gavin!

Gavin moves to DRC *to Stanley. Stanley is still sitting with his head in his hands*

Gavin I know but I came back to see Mr Smith. (*He points to Stanley*)
John (*to Stanley*) Mr Smith doesn't want to see you, do you, Mr Smith?

Stanley looks up, shakes his head dumbly and buries his head again

Gavin And I've decided to see Vicki after all.

Gavin sits on the R *arm of the settee*

John Gavin —— !
Gavin Look, I know she doesn't even know that I exist ——
John Discuss it at home!
Barbara What are you talking about, son? Vicki's just been over to Streatham.
John Barbara! (*He pushes Barbara to* DLC)
Gavin (*rising, delighted and surprised*) Vicki has?
Barbara (*crossing to Gavin*) She came especially to see you.
John Let's go!
Gavin No, I'll wait for her. This is great!

Gavin sits on the R arm of the settee

John No, it's not! (*Yelling across to Stanley*) Mr Smith, it's your turn to say
   something
Stanley I pass!
Barbara (*to Stanley*) Isn't your daughter here yet? She left ages before I did.
Gavin It'll probably take her some time to get back from Streatham. Even
   with her dog.
Barbara (*confused*) Her dog?
John (*yelling across*) Never goes anywhere without her dog, does she, Mr.
   Smith?!
Stanley (*blankly*) Dog, Mr Smith?

*John shuts his eyes and mimes "feeling the way". Stanley jumps up and
crosses to John DC below the settee*

   Oh, *that* dog! Yes, she just loves that dog. Won't leave home without
   Buster. (*To Gavin*) Well, she *can't* leave home without Buster, can she?
Gavin Hardly.
Stanley Lovely Buster!
John Lovely Buster!
Stanley ⎫
John ⎭ (*together, indicating*) ⎰ Tiny little thing with …
                                      ⎱ Great big Alsatian …

They stop and look at each other

Stanley ⎱
John   ⎰ (*together, indicating*) ⎰ Great big Alsatian …
                                       ⎱ Tiny little thing with …

They stop again and look at each other

John Sort of medium size, isn't she?
Stanley Yes, medium size.
John ⎫
Stanley ⎭ (*together*) Medium size.

   Dad enters from the kitchen

Dad I say! I've just put your dustbins out.

*During the following, Dad walks above the armchair, DRC, and collects his
stick*

Barbara (*to Gavin*) No, Vicki didn't have a dog with her.
Gavin She must have. She couldn't manage all the way to Streatham with just a white stick.

Barbara looks blank. Stanley walks away, sits in the armchair DLC and buries his head

Barbara A white stick?
Gavin She can't see!

Barbara crosses to Stanley

Barbara (*confused*) But, wait a minute — (*to Stanley*) — she arrived on a bicycle.

Stanley looks up

Stanley (*crying*) It's a computerized image.

Barbara and Gavin try to work this out

John She must be a game girl, that Vicki! Visually impaired but what guts!

John pulls Gavin across as Dad comes down to John's R

Dad (*to John*) Cor, I never knew that your Vicki was ——

John turns on Dad, furiously. Before John can do anything, Dad kicks his stick from under himself and falls to the floor. He immediately gets up and shadow boxes. He then goes UR to collect his stick. Mary starts to kick the second bedroom door. During the following, Dad wanders above the settee to DL

Mary (*off*) I'll kick this door in as well!
Gavin (*to Barbara*) Mrs Smith has to be locked in every afternoon.
John Thank you, Gavin!
Gavin (*to Barbara*) She makes Mr Smith sleep upstairs with Mr Gardner.
Barbara No!
John (*even more murderously*) Thank — you — Gavin!
Gavin (*to Stanley*) I suppose there'll be more room up there now Mr Gardner's died.
Barbara Died? (*She looks to Stanley*)

Stanley looks up, goes to speak then puts his hands on his head by way of submission

(*To Gavin*) Mr Gardner was upside-down doing yoga ten minutes ago.
John It doesn't matter!
Gavin No, Mr Gardner died right here. (*To Stanley*) Didn't he, Mr Smith?

Stanley puts his thumb in his mouth and curls up like a baby

John There's a perfectly simple explanation.

Barbara and Gavin look to him

(*Yelling across at Stanley*) So, for God's sake tell them, Mr Smith!

They look to Stanley. Stanley rocks himself like a baby for comfort. There is furious kicking from Mary

Mary (*off*) Hey!
John And quickly!

Stanley takes his thumb out of his mouth but stays curled up. His hysteria is only just below the surface

Stanley Anybody know the one about the dog and the vet?

The others look totally blank

(*Trying to control his hysteria*) A man goes to the vet. The vet says, "Your dog's died." The man says, "Ahhh" — so the vet opens his mouth.

They just stare at Stanley. Stanley's hysteria is nearing breaking point

The man's mouth, not the vet's mouth! (*He puts his thumb back in his mouth*)

Dad is now on Stanley's L

Dad (*laughing*) That's bloody funny, Stanley!

Stanley looks at Dad. Dad gives him the thumbs up and wanders to the stairs. John grabs Barbara and Gavin

John Barbara! Gavin! We're leaving! (*He pulls Barbara and Gavin* ULC *to the front door*)
Gavin Dad!
Barbara For heaven's sake, John.

John opens the front door

   Mary, looking maniacal and dishevelled, is standing in the doorway

Gavin hides behind Barbara as Mary marches in. The others watch agog as she picks up the carving knife from the table above settee

Mary (*to Stanley*) Right!
Dad Help! The hotel receptionist has gone mad. Police! Help!

   Dad exits hurriedly upstairs

Mary Now, Stanley Gardner!
Stanley (*leaping up*) Mary —— !
Mary That's twice I've had to climb out through a window! (*She moves towards Stanley with the knife*)

Stanley back away DL

Stanley Now, Mary ——
Mary (*pressing on*) If you're not out of here in five seconds, I'm going to cut your balls off. (*She advances on Stanley*)

Stanley protects himself

Stanley Mary!

Stanley runs in front of the settee to DR *followed by Mary*

John (*to Barbara*) I think this could get very bloody — and very high-pitched!

Mary moves above the armchair to DR *and points the knife at Stanley's "parts"*

Mary (*counting*) One!

Stanley runs below the armchair to DLC

Stanley (*as he goes*) Mary!

As Mary goes to chase Stanley, Barbara moves DRC *to Mary's* L

Barbara (*to Mary, quickly*) Bye, bye, Mary. It's been so nice to meet you.
I'm Mrs Smith. Gavin's Mum.

Mary is concentrating on Stanley

Mary   (*briefly*) Gavin's Mum. You've called at a very bad time! (*She
threatens Stanley across Barbara with the knife*)

Stanley retreats behind armchair DLC

Barbara (*sympathetically*) Yes, I know. You must try to hang on, though.

John hurries DLC *to below the settee*

John   (*to Barbara*) Just go!
Stanley Yes, just go!
Mary   (*aiming the knife across Barbara*) Two!

Gavin moves down to Barbara

Gavin   (*to Barbara*) Come on, let's go!
John   Yes!
Mary   (*to Gavin*) You're not still here! Do you want even more money?! (*She
crosses Barbara and backs Gavin to below the settee* C)
Gavin   (*nervously, at a loss*) Er — no.

John pulls Gavin across to DLC

John   No, he doesn't. (*To Stanley*) He doesn't want any more, does he?
Stanley No, he's satisfied ... (*Quickly*) He's had enough ... Just go!
Mary   (*to Stanley*) Three! (*She runs at Stanley*)

Stanley runs DL, *as John pushes Gavin up to the front door*

(*To Gavin*) Hey!

Gavin stops by the front door

How old are you?

Gavin Sixteen.
Mary (*to Stanley*) Sixteen! I thought so! (*She turns violently to Stanley with the knife*)
Stanley Mary! (*He runs across in front of settee to* DR *clutching his "parts"*)
Mary (*turns to Gavin*) Well, it's not too late to give girls a try.
Gavin (*confused*) Yeah. Sure.

Gavin exits via the front door

Mary moves in front of the settee to Barbara at DRC

Mary (*to Barbara*) You've got a son, haven't you?

Barbara looks surprised

Barbara Well — er — yes. "Gavin." (*She vaguely waves in the direction of the front door*)

John hurries DLC

John Nice name, "Gavin"!
Stanley Nice name, "Gavin"!

Stanley steps in. Mary crosses Barbara

Mary Four!

Stanley steps back

And how old is your Gavin?
Barbara (*to Mary*) Well — er ... (*She vaguely waves in the direction of the door*) He's sixteen.
Mary (*to Barbara*) Well, you look after your son!
John I'm sure she will!
Mary He's special!
John Yes, he's special!

John pulls Barbara away to DLC, *but Barbara returns to Mary*

Barbara (*to Mary; sympathetically*) Yes. Did you and Mr Smith lose a baby boy very early on?

Mary looks totally bemused. John walks to the kitchen door as Stanley steps to bedroom door. They lean their heads on the respective doors in despair

(*To Mary*) You mustn't blame yourself though. And it's not your fault either that your daughter is visually impaired.

Mary hesitates then, suddenly overcome, bursts into hysterical tears. The sudden screams make John and Stanley inadvertently bang their heads on the doors

John (*to Barbara*) Just leave her alone!
Stanley Yes, leave her alone!
Mary (*to Stanley; yelling through her tears*) Right! Five! (*She runs at Stanley with the knife aimed between his legs*)
Stanley Mary!!

Stanley runs up the stairs hotly pursued by John

John Come back!

Barbara moves URC *and holds Mary*

Barbara (*consoling Mary*) Mrs Smith! Don't!

Dad appears from upstairs

Dad Is it safe to come down now?
Stanley No, it's bloody not.

During the ensuing dialogue Barbara sits Mary, sobbing, on the settee

John (*grabbing Stanley*) I can't cope without you!
Stanley And I can't cope without me balls!
John Stanley!

Stanley exits quickly upstairs. In the process, he knocks Dad down the remaining stairs

Dad collects his towel and swimming trunks

Dad I'm going for a swim. If I'm not back by midnight, I'll be in Calais.

Dad exits through the kitchen

John, very nervously, moves to above the armchair DLC *watching Mary and Barbara intensely*

Barbara (*to Mary*) There, there!

Mary He should stay upstairs where he bloody-well belongs.

Barbara No, everything will be all right. And you don't really want to cut his ——

Mary (*interrupting*) Yes, I bloody do! (*She rises and moves to chase Stanley*)

Barbara rises and stops Mary

Barbara He's doing his best for you, Mrs Smith. (*She takes the knife from Mary*) He loves you.

Mary (*staring at Barbara*) What?

Barbara sits with Mary on the settee. Barbara on the R and Mary on the L. John, very worried, steps in a pace

Barbara He *loves* you. (*She leans over and puts the knife on the table behind the settee*) Do you know what you should do?

Mary (*flatly*) What?

Barbara Tell him to stop sleeping upstairs and jump into *your* bed.

Mary looks appalled

John I don't think that's a very good idea. (*He goes to pull Mary up*)

Mary resists

Mary (*to Barbara, pointing upstairs*) That lay-about, in my bed?!

Barbara A nightly session of sex will cure most things.

Mary hesitates then breaks into hysterical screams again. She rises and crosses Barbara. Barbara rises and re-sits next to Mary. Mary is now on the R and Barbara is on the L of the settee

John (*to Barbara*) I don't think Mrs Smith is into alternative medicine.

John lifts Barbara up

Mary (*rising*) No! (*To Barbara*) Would *you* jump into bed with *your* lodger?!

Barbara (*taken aback*) Well, no I wouldn't.

Mary Then don't tell me to do it with Stanley bloody Gardner!

Barbara (*confused*) Stanley —— ?

John (*interrupting; to Barbara*) Time to go, Mrs Smith! (*He tries to pull Barbara away*)

Barbara resists and sits back with Mary

Barbara (*to Mary; laughing*) No, you misunderstood. I was saying you
  should sleep with your *husband*. Him! (*She turns and points upstairs*)
Mary I'm not married to that useless bugger up there.
John (*frantically*) Anybody know the one about the dog and the vet?
Mary I'm married to *him*. (*She points across Barbara to John*)

*There is a pause, then Barbara turns and looks to John. There is a moment's
awful pause*

  Dad enters from kitchen still clutching a towel

Dad I asked four people!! And not one of them knew the way to the beach.
John (*trying to contain his hysteria*) This dog takes a man to the vet. The vet
  says "Ahhh" and opens his mouth; so the man puts the dog in it!

Mary and Barbara continue to stare at John

  (*Frantically*) This lady takes her pussy to the vet. The vet says to the
  pussy ... (*He stops*) Pussy — pussy — pussy.
Dad It's the way you tell 'em.
John It's the way I tell 'em all right. OK, OK, I've had a good run! The game
  is finally up. (*He takes a breath and during the following moves above the
  settee and to* DRC) What I'm going to say will surprise you both — well,
  more than surprise you. Mr Gardner, will you sit down, please.
Dad All right. I hope this one's funnier than your others.

Dad sits in the armchair DLC

John (*simply and seriously*) It's not funny at all actually. (*To Mary and
  Barbara*) I love you.

Mary and Barbara just nod in unison

  Our marriage has been wonderful — perfect — fantastic.

Mary and Barbara just nod in unison

  I don't think I can live without you.

Mary and Barbara just nod in unison

  Either of you.

Mary and Barbara start to nod — but then look to each other for a moment.
They then look back to John

That's it, really. Oh, yes. I'm married to both of you.

Mary and Barbara just look at John

Well, there we are! I'll — er — move out today, Mary. And I'll move out
from Streatham as well, Barbara. I suppose the police will have to be told
— criminal offence. (*Tenderly*) I just want to say thanks for everything —
thanks for the KitKats and the Mars Bars, Mary, and all the super soups and
the lamb stews. And thanks for all the vegetarian meals and health food
stuff, Barbara. And, well — I'm sorry.

John, overcome, sits in the armchair DRC and puts his head in his hands. Mary
and Barbara just look at him. Dad rises

Dad If that's the funniest you've got I'm going for a swim.

Dad exits into kitchen with his towel and costume

There is a pause. Then Mary and Barbara laugh

Mary (*laughing; to Barbara*) You tell him.
Barbara (*laughing*) OK. (*She looks to John*) Johnny, we've known for
years.

There is a brief pause and then John slowly looks up. Mary and Barbara grin
happily and warmly at John

John (*blankly*) You've known for ——?
Mary — about fifteen years.
John (*rising*) Fifteen ——?!

During the following, Mary and Barbara, still chuckling, walk to either side
of John and take an arm each, Mary on John's L and Barbara on his R

Barbara (*rising*) We're not stupid, pumpkin.
Mary (*rising*) All those dreadful excuses, Johnny.
Barbara And then week after week after week ——
John What?
Mary "Not tonight, I'm too tired."
Barbara But you know what your biggest mistake is, sweetheart?
John What?

Mary ⎫
Barbara ⎰ (*together*) You talk in your sleep!

They both kiss John on the cheek and hug him

Barbara (*saucily*) So one day I followed you ——
John (*with outrage*) Barbara!
Mary (*saucily*) And then I followed you ——
John Mary!
Barbara That's how we met.
Mary And we decided we'd got it pretty good.
Barbara Yes. You weren't cluttering up the house too often.
Mary You spoilt us rotten so we wouldn't suspect.
Barbara And it was fun comparing notes.
John Wait a minute! Wait a minute! Whoa-whoa-whoa! If you've known all along, (*to Mary*) why were you having screaming hysterics just now? (*To Barbara*) And why were you comforting her and giving her advice?

During the following, Mary and Barbara can hardly contain their laughter

Barbara We were trying to spin it out as long as possible.
Mary We haven't had so much fun in years.
Barbara We've had some laughs since we found out. But, I reckon that today was the best. (*To Mary*) Don't you?
Mary Definitely.
John (*astounded*) And you've both known for fifteen years?

Still laughing, Mary and Barbara nod. John looks at them for a moment

(*Sternly*) I think your behaviour is the most deceitful, despicable, betrayal of a marriage ——

Mary and Barbara step back and point a derisive finger at him: interrupting and laughing at his effrontery

Mary ⎫
Barbara ⎰ (*together*) Oh!
John (*pressing on*) — of all the sly, underhand, conniving ——

Mary and Barbara step back to John and put their arms around him. They kiss him

Stanley enters purposefully down the stairs carrying his suitcase. He is now dressed. He marches DLC

Stanley Right, I'm off! Where's Dad?
John (*still angry*) Stanley, I think there's something you should know ——
Stanley (*interrupting*) No! I'm going on holiday with my father. I'm not helping you any more!
John Stanley, it's all right!

Stanley moves below C settee

Stanley No! If you think I'm hanging around here to be castrated by Mary ... (*He stops; blankly*) Mary and Barbara are cuddling you.
John Yes!
Stanley They've got happy smiling faces.
John Yes!

There is a pause

Stanley Wake up, Stanley, wake up! (*He walks away to* DLC *smacking his cheeks*)

John crosses to below the settee, C

John They've known for fifteen years!
Stanley God, I've had a half a dozen heart attacks for nothing. (*He sits in the armchair* DLC)

Vicki hurries in to DLC, *through the front door*

Vicki I've just met Gavin down the road!

They all turn to Vicki

He's fantastic! He's so *polite*, I mean, *considerate*. He took me by the arm. He escorted me across the road. He said, "Mind the pavement." "Watch where you're going."

John moves to Vicki

John (*gently*) Vicki ——
Vicki (*pressing on*) I really like him, Dad. He's as sexy as hell!
John Vicki.
Vicki (*pressing on*) He's asked me to go to this club with him tonight. And he wants to take me on his motorbike to Brighton.
John Vicki —— !

Vicki He's brilliant! And he wants to buy me a dog!
John (*simply*) Vicki, you mustn't see him any more.
Vicki Don't start that again!
John No, Vicki, please —— !
Vicki Listen, I *like* him! That's all. I'm not saying, I'm going to sleep with him and make babies!
John Vicki!
Vicki But we will if we want to.

Vicki runs out

John Vicki! Mary, I've got to tell her!

John goes to move, but Mary quickly steps in and stops him

Mary No, don't!
John I must!
Mary No, you mustn't!
John Mary! There's no future for them! They've both got the same father!
Mary No, they haven't!

There is a pause as John takes this in. Mary quickly sits them both on the settee. Barbara sits in the armchair DRC

Mary (*rapidly*) You're not Vicki's father. I'm sorry, Johnny. It was only once. Sixteen years ago. I was alone a lot. Feeling — you know. It was only once.
John (*bravely*) Who was it?
Mary The lodger.

Mary points across John to Stanley. John looks at Stanley. Stanley stands up, mortified. He then indicates to John it was only "once" by raising one finger. John picks up the knife from the table behind the settee. Stanley is rooted to the spot

Stanley John! It was only once! Once! You've been unfaithful every other night for eighteen years.

John rises, "weighing up" the knife. Stanley holds his "parts". John slowly advances upon Stanley

John, don't! I'll pay all the back rent! I've been a good friend, John! Except for once. I've been a good friend!

John (*suddenly grinning*) You've been a fantastic friend, mate! (*He throws the knife down and hugs Stanley*)

Stanley is amazed

Stanley Wake up, Stanley, wake up! (*He madly slaps his own cheeks again and moves* DL)

During the following, John crosses to Mary and Barbara, and hugs them

John I must be the luckiest man in the world. A great mate. Two lovely wives. Two lovely kids. They'll have lovely kids. Life's brilliant!

Dad enters from the kitchen with his stick. He is wearing his "Long-John" underpants with his bathing trunks over them

Dad (*as he enters*) This hotel's miles from the beach, you know.

Everybody laughs. Stanley starts to kiss and cuddle Dad. Dad tries to fight him off

Music

Black-out

The CURTAIN *falls*

FURNITURE AND PROPERTY LIST

ACT I

On Stage: Hall stand with hooks. *On hooks*: coats, leather motor-bike jacket
Settee, with large cotton throw
Two armchairs
Small chest of drawers
Small table
Mirror
In cupboard under stairs L: Coats, **John's** jacket, anorak, hats and
    scarfs, **Vicki's** crash helmet
Keys in the locks of all room doors
Narrow table
Small chair
Rug??
Small table L. *On it*: telephone with long lead
Small table R. *On it*: cordless telephone
Pictures, prints, plants as dressing

Off stage: Computer print-out (**Gavin**)
Computer print-out (**Vicki**)
Lunch-box (**Mary**)
Two large shopping bags containing a sun hat, sun cream, mosquito
    repellent, Imodium Plus, snorkel, mask, water wings, rubber bath-
    ing cap, car-keys (**Stanley**)
Two flasks (**Mary**)
Mug of tea (**Mary**)
Mug of tea (**Mary**)
Crash helmet (**Gavin**)
Glass of water, bottle of aspirins (**Mary**)
Empty glass (**Mary**)
Large saucepan (**Mary**)
Shoulder bag (**Vicki**)
Bicycle (**Vicki**)
Pile of plates and cutlery (**Mary**)
Kitchen gloves, dish of steaming vegetables (**Mary**)

Personal: **John**: mobile phone

ACT II

On stage: As Act I
        On table ULC: newspaper

Off stage: Suitcase, heavy duty metal stick (or Zimmer frame) (**Dad**)
        Shoulder-bag(**Vicki**)
        Glass of juice (**Barbara**)
        Loaf of bread on bread board (**Mary**)
        Bicycle (**Vicki**)
        Glass of whisky (**Mary**)
        Carving knife (**Mary**)
        Bed sheet (**Gavin**)
        Medicine bottle (**Mary**)
        Rolled-up towel containing swimming trunks (**Dad**)
        Suitcase (**Stanley**)

Personal: **Stanley**: five pound note
        Vicki: lipstick
        John: sunglasses

LIGHTING PLOT

Property fitting required: nil
Interior. The same throughout

ACT I

To open: Mid-afternoon. Warm summer's day effect

Cue 1	Music	(Page 56)
	Black-out	

ACT II

To open: Mid-afternoon. Warm summer's day effect

Cue 2	Music	(Page 113)
	Black-out	

EFFECTS PLOT

N.B. The Wimbledon doorbell and phone ring L, should sound different to the Streatham doorbell and phone ring R. John's mobile telephone plays a merry march tune.

ACT I

Cue 13	**Stanley** gives **Vicki** a little wave *The Wimbledon phone rings*	(Page 26)
Cue 14	**Stanley**: "All right, all right!" **John**'s *mobile rings*	(Page 28)
Cue 15	**Mary** moves to the second bedroom door *Sound of* **Gavin**'s *motorbike starting up*	(Page 32)
Cue 16	**Stanley**: "John! John! Your mobile." *Sound of car pulling away with screech of tyres*	(Page 33)
Cue 17	**Stanley** swims the breast stroke **John**'s *mobile rings*	(Page 34)
Cue 18	**Stanley** leans against the door, exhausted *The Wimbledon front doorbell rings*	(Page 38)
Cue 19	**Stanley** slams the door and leans against it *The Wimbledon front doorbell rings*	(Page 38)
Cue 20	**Stanley**: "That's a very fair question." *The Wimbledon front doorbell rings*	(Page 39)
Cue 21	**Stanley** hesitates *The Wimbledon front doorbell rings*	(Page 39)
Cue 22	**Stanley** closes his eyes and looks up *The Wimbledon front doorbell rings*	(Page 39)
Cue 23	**Stanley** tiptoes towards the second bedroom **John**'s *mobile rings*	(Page 45)
Cue 24	**Barbara** moves towards the front door *The Streatham phone rings*	(Page 48)
Cue 25	**John** does a breaststroke towards the front door *The Wimbledon doorbell gives a long urgent ring*	(Page 55)
Cue 26	**John** stops in front of the settee *The Wimbledon doorbell rings*	(Page 56)
Cue 27	**John** holds his nose, jumps and sinks to the floor *Music*	(Page 56)

ACT II

Cue 43   **John** decides on the kitchen door   (Page 85)
               The Wimbledon doorbell rings

Cue 44   **John**: "I got rid of them."   (Page 86)
               The Wimbledon doorbell rings

Cue 45   **Dad**: "... wits about you, Stanley"   (Page 87)
               The Wimbledon doorbell rings

Cue 46   **Stanley**: "Go upstairs!"   (Page 87)
               The Wimbledon doorbell rings

Cue 47   **John**: " ... dealing with Gavin and Mary."   (Page 87)
               The Wimbledon doorbell rings urgently

Cue 48   **Stanley**: "... like a shot."   (Page 95)
               The main bedroom door is splintered with a crash

Cue 49   **Dad** exits   (Page 98)
               Extended sound of crashing crockery and saucepans

Cue 50   **Dad** fights **Stanley** off   (Page 113)
               Music
